Praise for *Humble Roots*

This is an exquisite book. In *Humble Roots*, Hannah Anderson intends to make us gardeners . . . to plant and tend that rarest of cultivars, humility. Humility orients us rightly toward our bodies, emotions, and intellect. It orients us rightly toward our possessions, desires, and circumstances. It orients us rightly toward the cross. And nurtured carefully in the fertile soil of grace, humility grants us a harvest of true rest. Wistful, nostalgic, and deeply wise. I read it through tears.

JEN WILKIN
Bible teacher and author of *Women of the Word* and *None Like Him*

Hannah's use of the gardening metaphor was so beautiful that I started to long for a rural home where I could can my own green beans or pick blackberries. *Humble Roots* is a concise invitation (without how-tos) to put off the pride of accomplishment, self-trust, and works righteousness, and enter into the humility that is not only the door to true Christianity but also the daily life of deep faith.

ELYSE M. FITZPATRICK
Author of *Home: How Heaven and the New Earth Satisfy Our Deepest Longings*

A beautiful, poignant, and wise book. You will see connections between God's world and His Word that you have never noticed: between tomatoes and impatience, honey and competitiveness, soil and resurrection. And if you're anything like me, you will find yourself rejoicing.

ANDREW WILSON
Teaching Pastor at King's Church London
Author of *The Life We Never Expected* and *Unbreakable*

Hannah Anderson takes being a locavore even more seriously than farm-to-table restaurants and farmer's market goers. She takes it to the most local place of all: our own hearts. This is the book I've been wanting on the shelves of Christians everywhere.

LORE FERGUSON WILBERT
Writer at Sayable.net, *Christianity Today*, Revive our Hearts, She Reads Truth, and more

God made us to be close to the ground. So it's fitting that Hannah Anderson roots her clear and compassionate teaching in stories close to the ground. The result is nourishment for our souls. Anderson replants us in the Father's provision, wisdom, and care.

KATELYN BEATY
Managing Editor, *Christianity Today* magazine
Author of *A Woman's Place*

C. S. Lewis famously wrote that humility is not thinking less of ourselves; rather, it is thinking of ourselves less, and in such a way that frees us to redirect our energies toward God and those He has given us to love. Using one of God's favorite places and metaphors, the garden, coupled with endearing and sometimes humbling anecdotes from her own life story, Hannah paints a compelling picture of why we should, and ways that we can, pour contempt on our pride. Please read this book. It will renew your perspective, and it could change your life.

SCOTT SAULS
Senior Pastor, Christ Presbyterian Church, Nashville, TN
Author of *Jesus Outside the Lines* **and** *Befriend*

Hannah has written a simple but profound book. Her earthy style of writing accents the deep truths of Scripture in a way that is accessible to those of us who most need to hear this message. I predict this book will become a classic on the subject.

WENDY ALSUP
Author of *Practical Theology for Women* and *The Gospel-Centered Woman*
Blogger at www.theologyforwomen.org

This is just the kind of book I love: readers are promised a meal—and *Humble Roots* delivers a feast. With serious biblical reflection and vivid storytelling, Hannah Anderson compels us to seek humility. Rooted in Jesus, we abandon our illusions of control; we embrace our limits; we learn to *depend*.

JEN POLLOCK MICHEL
Author of *Teach Us to Want*, *Christianity Today*'s 2015 Book of the Year

Humble Roots is soulful spirituality at its best—earthy, embodied, and energizing. Anderson beckons us to reconsider both the rhythms of God's creation and the frantic pace of our lives. The gospel brings reconciliation of all things in heaven and earth. This includes our God-formed bodies to the land God created for us.

DANIEL MONTGOMERY
Lead Pastor, Sojourn Community Church, Louisville, KY;
founder of the Sojourn Network
Author of *Faithmapping, PROOF*, and *Leadership Mosaic*

I can think of nothing that might fix what ails this increasingly chaotic, power-hungry world more than a dose of humility and deeper rootedness. Whether you're a city slicker, a suburban dweller, or a country bumpkin, these true parables—lovely memories of rural life seasoned with sharp insights—will hit you right where you live.

KAREN SWALLOW PRIOR
Author of *Booked: Literature in the Soul of Me* and *Fierce Convictions: The Extraordinary Life of Hannah More: Poet, Reformer, Abolitionist*

HUMBLE ROOTS

---

*How Humility
Grounds
and Nourishes
Your Soul*

HANNAH ANDERSON

MOODY PUBLISHERS

CHICAGO

Unless otherwise indicated, Scripture quotations are from the ESV® Bible (The Holy Bible, English Standard Version®), copyright © 2001 by Crossway, a publishing ministry of Good News Publishers. Used by permission. All rights reserved.

Scripture quotations marked KJV are taken from the King James Version.

Emphasis to Scripture has been added by the author.

Published in association with the literary agency of Wolgemuth & Associates, Inc.

Edited by Pam Pugh
Interior design: Erik M. Peterson
Illustrator: Michelle Berg Radford
Author photo: Mary Wall
Cover Design: Faceout Studio
Cover image of wild plants copyright © by Potapov Alexander / Shutterstock (152430485).
  of herbs copyright © by Thumbelina / Shutterstock (132140750).
  of texture copyright © by donatas1205 / Shutterstock (48954079).
  All rights reserved for all images.

Library of Congress Cataloging-in-Publication Data

Names: Anderson, Hannah, 1979- author.
Title: Humble roots : how humility grounds and nourishes your soul / Hannah Anderson.
Description: Chicago : Moody Publishers, [2016]
Identifiers: LCCN 2016019854 (print) | LCCN 2016029563 (ebook) | ISBN 9780802414595 | ISBN 9780802494450 ()
Subjects: LCSH: Humility--Religious aspects--Christianity.
Classification: LCC BV4647.H8 A525 2016 (print) | LCC BV4647.H8 (ebook) | DDC 241/.4--dc23
LC record available at https://lccn.loc.gov/2016019854

ISBN: 978-0-8024-1459-5

We hope you enjoy this book from Moody Publishers. Our goal is to provide high-quality, thought-provoking books and products that connect truth to your real needs and challenges. For more information on other books and products written and produced from a biblical perspective, go to www.moodypublishers.com or write to:

Moody Publishers
820 N. LaSalle Boulevard
Chicago, IL 60610

5 7 9 10 8 6 4

Printed in the United States of America

For

Ruth Evelyn

and

Stella Marie

whose humble roots have run deep
and whose lives have produced
abundant fruit

Contents

Sowing Seeds

I didn't know how much I needed to read this book until after I'd written it.

Like many of you, I am in the throes of responsible adulthood—my days spent caring for family, serving the church, and pursuing good work. And just like many of you, I often find myself overwhelmed by these good things. I wouldn't change any of them, but I do regularly feel worn out, anxious about my abilities, and caught in cycles of comparison and perfectionism. To use Jesus' words, I regularly feel "heavy laden."

For years, I've heard that the solution to such stress comes from setting up boundaries, finding ways to be more productive, cultivating gratitude, and scheduling "me-time." For years, I've believed that finding rest comes from both simultaneously learning to let go and keeping your act together. For years, I've thought that my sense of peace depends entirely on me.

In Matthew 11:28, Jesus invites tired, weary people—people like us—to come to Him. "Come to me, all who labor, and are heavy laden, and I will give you rest," He promises. But then, He continues in a most unexpected way. "Take my yoke upon you, and learn from me, *for I am gentle and lowly in heart*, and you will find rest for your souls." In other words, peace doesn't start with me; peace starts with Him.

Even more surprisingly, peace starts with learning His humility. *There's something here*, I thought as I read Jesus' words one day. *This is important. This is something different entirely.*

But despite having an inkling, I still didn't totally understand what Jesus meant. I knew that the way we usually talk about coping with stress and anxiety wasn't sufficient, but I still couldn't see the whole picture. So I did what any author would do in this situation: I decided to write a book.

When a family friend heard this, he asked what the book would be about.

"Well, it's kind of—well you know . . ." I began, stumbling through the elevator pitch that authors are supposed to have memorized, ready to share at a moment's notice. "It's about how we're all so anxious and busy and we, um, well, we think we can do everything and we try to save the world. And, um, I think there's a connection. I think something's wrong. Like . . . um . . . we're stressed out because we're trying to do too much . . . and um, well maybe we just need to learn to be human again. I think maybe we need to learn humility."

"Oh, I can write that book for you," he said confidently. "In fact, I can write it in three words: You're. Not. God." And with those three words he summed up what would eventually take me fifty thousand.

You're not God. I'm not God. None of us are God.

But how often and how easily we forget this! How often we try to live beyond normal human limits. How often we try to do it all, to know it all, to be it all. And how often we end up stressed, anxious, and overwhelmed because of it. To be fair, it's a subtle dilemma, one that can hide behind an honest desire to do good and make a difference in the world. Because human beings are made in God's image, it's natural that we end up looking and acting a lot like Him. As we mature in faith, we strive to become more loving, more gracious, more wise, and even more productive. But as we do, we must never forget that looking like God does not mean that we are God. We are made in His image, but we are *made* nonetheless.

In many ways, *Humble Roots* continues a conversation that started in a book I wrote a few years ago. That book, *Made for More*, explores the doctrine of *imago dei* or what it means to be made in God's image. Instead of finding identity in our roles—in being fathers and mothers, teachers and writers and pastors—we must find identity in being image bearers of God. But upon reading *Made for More*, my friend Amy asked, and rightly so, "Okay, how do we live out this lofty vision? What is the way forward . . . where do we go from here?"

At the risk of oversimplification, we live out this vision, we live as image bearers, the same way we began: humbly dependent on our Creator. We live it out, yes, by learning to "do justice and to love kindness" as the prophet Micah commands us; but we also live it out by learning to "walk humbly with your God."[1]

In other words, the humility that brings us rest is the same humility that frees us to be the people God created us to be.

In *Humble Roots*, we'll explore the theological truths of incarnation, creaturehood, physical embodiment, and human limitation; and we'll do this by considering the natural world around us, by lifting our eyes to the hills, the fields, and the heavens. But we'll also consider more practical questions about how humility informs our daily choices—ones that generally take place in less idyllic settings. We'll see how humility—how knowing ourselves as creatures—also helps us see the extent of our pride in our everyday choices, from how we use social media to how we give and receive compliments. But more than simply pointing out where

---

1. Micah 6:8.

we fail, humility also provides a way forward. Humility frees us to flourish as the human beings we were made to be: to celebrate the goodness of our physical bodies, to embrace the complexity of our emotions, and to own our unique gifts without guilt or feeling like an imposter.

Humble Roots is not a sequel to *Made for More*, but it is the other half of the conversation. At the same time, it's also a conversation all its own, one that can be explored and savored for its own sake. If, however, you have read *Made for More* and it inspired you to think about yourself as a person destined to reflect God, *Humble Roots* will help you think about yourself as a person dependent on God to do just that. And remembering this simple but essential reality—that "You're not God"—will lead to the spiritual and emotional rest you long for.

A few points of order before we begin, though. The goal of *Humble Roots* is to understand how pride manifests itself in anxiety and restlessness; and how humility frees us from the cycle of stress, performance, and competition. In this sense, it is primarily a theological reflection, and you should use it as such. *Humble Roots* is not intended to replace the God-given graces of community, pastoral counsel, professional therapy, and when necessary, medical intervention. If you are experiencing debilitating physical or mental issues associated with clinical anxiety or depression, please seek the help of trusted friends, clergy, and mental health professionals. They are God's gifts to us, His broken, hurting children, and we humbly receive them as such.

And second, many of the stories and illustrations in this book are personal. The title, *Humble Roots*, alludes to both how the natural world teaches us humble dependence on God and how I am learning these lessons through the people and places He has ordained for my life. I chose to use personal examples because this is how I am encountering these truths every day. But in order to protect the people in my community, I have changed names and altered identifying details. We tend to live life out of the limelight and that is exactly how we'd like it to continue.

"Have this mind among yourselves," the apostle Paul writes in Philippians 2:5–8, "which is yours in Christ Jesus, who, though he was in the form of God, did not count equality with God a thing to be grasped, but emptied himself, taking the form of a servant, being born in the likeness of men. And being found in human form, he humbled himself . . ."

> *"Learn from me for I am gentle and lowly in heart . . . "*
> *"Have this mind among yourselves which is yours in Christ Jesus . . ."*
> *"Being found in human form, he humbled himself . . ."*

Yes, there is something here. Something rich and restful. Something true and beautiful. Something that will lead us to flourishing and peace.

I

They shall sit every man under his vine
and under his fig tree, and no one shall
make them afraid, for the mouth of the
LORD of hosts has spoken.

—MICAH 4:4

FIGURE 1

Red Anemone, *Anemone coronaria*

Withering on the Vine

*"The kind of life that makes one feel empty and shallow
and superficial, that makes one dread to read and dread to
think, can't be good for one, can it? It can't be the kind of
life one was meant to live."* —*Willa Cather*

I was done. I had reached my limit.

I rolled over to check the time—1:26 a.m.—and then rolled
back over to look at my husband. By the light of the waxing
moon, I could just make out the shape of his body under the white
matelasse quilt we shared; his eyes were closed, his head resting se-
renely on his pillow. As my eyes adjusted to the silver-blue light,
I could also see that his cotton pillowcase had a dark smudge on
it—the consequence of having three children who love to cuddle
and having made chocolate no-bake cookies earlier in the day. *Remember to strip the bed in the morning and put a load in the washer
before you make breakfast*, I instructed myself, knowing full well
that I wouldn't.

I looked back at my husband who lay there facing me, although
not seeing me. His entire body was relaxed, his arm draped across
his bare chest, one hand extending in my direction and the other
tucked beneath his head in an almost childlike posture. His

breathing was heavy but unrushed, rhythmic and content. The breathing of a man at rest. The breathing of a man oblivious to the fact that he was sleeping on a chocolate-stained pillowcase.

This wasn't the first time I'd found myself wide awake while everyone else in the house was asleep. If anything, it seemed to be happening more and more often despite the fact that all my children were past the nighttime feedings of infancy and soaked sheets of the toddler years. When one of them did need me, they'd simply stumble into our bed, dragging their blankets and stuffed menagerie with them. There was little reason for me to be awake at 1:26 a.m.

But there I lay: restless while everyone else rested.

To make matters worse, I was finding that my agitation didn't limit itself to nighttime hours. During the day, my mind raced from one responsibility to the next, mentally calculating all the things I needed to accomplish before bed. It also kept track of how many calories I'd consumed, what chores I'd left undone, and my failures to be an appropriately invested mother, readily available friend, and consistently devoted wife. And all of it made me so very tired.

I was tired of feeling judged everywhere I turned—unfinished to-do lists, neglected friendships, unreturned voicemails, and looming deadlines. I was tired of feeling overworked, tired of being stressed out, tired from all the busyness. I was tired of being sensitive, fragile, and snippy. I was also tired of knowing that I had absolutely no right to feel the way I did.

Blessed?

Despite my restlessness, our family was in the middle of one of the most blessed, most productive times of our lives. For many years of our married life, we'd existed in crisis mode: young babies, un-

and underemployment, issues at church, and multiple job transitions. But recently, Nathan had landed his dream job as a pastor of a small church in Appalachia, less than an hour from where he'd grown up. Like Edward Ferrars in the 1995 screen adaptation of *Sense and Sensibility*, my husband wanted nothing more than "a small parish where [he] might do some good. Keep chickens. Give very short sermons."[1] So after eleven years of marriage—and almost as many moves—we returned to his home, to his Virginia, bought our first house, and started to put down roots. The move itself wasn't too difficult for me because I'd grown up in a similar community in the Pennsylvania foothills. I understood the cultural rhythms and loved the intimacy of smaller congregations. As a family, we were also moving into a new phase: Our children were quickly becoming self-reliant and nary a diaper, jar of baby food, or backward-facing car seat was in sight. To top it off, I'd just published a book. By anyone's standards, we were experiencing a new level of financial, physical, and professional freedom.

But still I felt weighed down.

For a while, I chalked it up to the stress of moving, the adjustment of living in yet another new place, meeting new people, and settling in.

It's a busy season . . .

If we can just get through this week, next week will be easier . . .

Maybe I need a girls' night out or a vacation . . .

If everyone would stop asking me to do stuff, I'd be okay . . . .

But eventually, like the excuse of motherhood, these excuses wore thin too. Time passed, we developed a routine, but I still felt overwhelmed. The work I accomplished each day never felt like enough, and I regularly crawled into bed feeling like a failure. Some

1. Despite being a memorable line, this exact wording is not in Jane Austen's original work, which was published in 1811.

nights, as I lay awake next to my husband, I wondered whether I really wanted to sleep after all: I'd simply have to wake up the next morning and start the cycle all over again.

Nathan, on the other hand, seemed to experience a natural (and infuriating) calm. He'd come home from the church, change out of his dress clothes, and work around the house. He'd play or do homework with the kids, putter in his garden, split firewood for the coming winter, and eventually, when it was time for bed, lay his head on his pillow and drift into an effortless eight hours of rest.

"How do you do that?" I asked him once. "How do you just go off to sleep the way you do?"

He looked at me with the same blank stare he might have offered if I'd asked him to stand on his head and recite the Etruscan alphabet. I persisted.

"I mean, how do you turn it all off? How do you just lie down and . . . fall asleep?"

"It's not that complicated, really. I'm tired. I lay down. I close my eyes. I go to sleep."

"Well, I'm tired too, but my mind just keeps turning—I keep thinking about all the stuff I didn't get done and the stuff I'll have to do when I wake up and to remember to take the kids to piano lessons and email my editor and call Nancy to see how her surgery went—"

"That's because you're an A-plus kind of girl, Hannah," he interrupted. "Me? I'm content with a B-plus. Just go to sleep."

Was it that? Was I simply a perfectionist? I didn't feel like a perfectionist—my house certainly didn't scream "perfectionist." It screamed a lot of other things, but it didn't scream perfect. When I thought about the piles of clothes sitting next to the washer, I'd feel guilty. But when I began working through the piles, sorting them into darks and whites, heavy and light, I'd feel guilty over owning so much stuff. And then I'd feel guilty about feeling guilty.

No, I wasn't a perfectionist. I was simply losing my mind.

Age of Anxiety

But, of course, I wasn't. Losing my mind would have been a legitimate explanation for the level of angst I was experiencing; embarrassingly, my troubles were much more mundane. The truth was that I had no large looming problems, only small ones that *felt* large. I had no major life crises, only minor ones that *felt* major. I had no monumental difficulties, only trivial ones that *felt* unbelievably monumental. I was stressed and unhappy with a very normal life.

As it turns out, I am not the only one to feel this way. In 2015, the American Psychological Association released a report detailing the state of stress in the United States. The purpose of the study was to measure "attitudes and perceptions of stress among the general public . . . and draw attention to the serious physical and emotional implications of stress and the inextricable link between the mind and body."[2] In other words, the APA was trying to figure out why so many of us spent our days feeling overwhelmed and unable to sleep at night.

According to the data, 75 percent of Americans report experiencing some level of stress in the previous month, with 42 percent reporting that they had lain awake at night and 33 percent reporting that they had eaten unhealthy food as a result. And while the sources of our stress are varied—money, work, family responsibilities, and physical health—my own experience suggests that some of us are skillful enough to worry about all of these things at the same time.

And when we do, we end up irritable, nervous, apathetic, fatigued, and overwhelmed. In her book *The Happiness Project*, Gretchen Rubin described her own experience with stress this way:

2. "Paying With Our Health," American Psychological Association. February 4, 2015, https://www.apa.org/news/press/releases/stress/2014/stress-report.pdf.

I had much to be happy about . . . but too often I sniped at my husband. . . . I felt dejected after even a minor professional setback. I drifted out of touch with old friends, I lost my temper easily, I suffered bouts of melancholy, insecurity, listlessness, and free-floating.[3]

The data also suggests that Ms. Rubin's being a woman and a mother made her particularly susceptible to experiencing higher incidence of stress. Compared to men, women report higher levels of stress, and compared to their childless peers, parents report higher levels of stress as well. For some, the data is even more unsettling. If you happen to be a woman, a mother, and part of the Millennial generation, your vulnerability to stress is even greater. It appears that the carefree days of youth are no longer carefree. Whether it's the struggle to find stable employment or finally having to face the realities of the world apart from hovering parents, young adults report higher rates of stress and depression than older adults do.

Truthfully, we don't need a report to tell us how much anxiety is creeping into the corners of our lives. When I run into a friend in our small community, we inevitably end up commiserating about how busy we are and how we can't get things done and we'll have to get together soon but of course we won't. At church, the conversations are the same: "I'd love to help, but I just can't right now."

So when I see these statistics, I don't see numbers; I see people. I see moms and dads and grandmas and grandpas who stand in the pick-up line with me every Monday through Friday at 2:20 waiting to shuttle our kids to the next scheduled event. I see my younger friends who are trying to sort out where they belong in this

---

3. Gretchen Rubin, *The Happiness Project: Or Why I Spent a Year Trying to Sing in the Morning, Clean My Closets, Fight Right, Read Aristotle, and Generally Have More Fun* (New York: Harper, 2009), 1–2.

world while the world taps its toes, demanding that they hurry up and figure it out. I see peers in ministry, freely giving of their time and energy but privately wondering whether their efforts amount to anything. I see women and men whose social media feeds flood with image after perfect image, but who never see the less than perfect backdrops behind them.

I see all of us: blessed beyond measure, but exhausted, anxious, and uncertain nonetheless.

The Lilies of the Field

"Consider the lilies of the field, how they grow: they neither toil nor spin, yet I tell you, even Solomon in all his glory was not arrayed like one of these." —Jesus of Nazareth

One February, several years ago, I unexpectedly found myself sitting on a hillside in the southern Golan Heights, near the Sea of Galilee. It wasn't entirely unexpected, of course. Nathan and I had planned the trip, bought tickets, boarded a plane in Philadelphia, and were subsequently welcomed by friends in Tel Aviv's Ben Gurion Airport. For the next week, we wandered the ancient alleyways of Jaffa, got caught in a rare storm in the En Gedi, jostled through Jerusalem's stalls and shrines, and eventually made it to the more peaceful environs of Galilee. Still, finding myself sitting on that hillside was unexpected in the sense that I'd never known to dream of the possibility.

But there I was. And at my feet lay a silvery lake, rimmed by neat olive groves and vineyards, rectangular fields of the kibbutzim, and clusters of small towns. Oddly enough, from my vantage point 450 meters above the sea's northeastern border, the view reminded me of home. The kibbutzim could have easily been dairy farms or small family homesteads; the olive trees and vineyards, exotic counterparts to mountaintop orchards and grape arbors; and if I squinted just right, the rolling hills could have been the hills that surrounded our house. The small towns, too, would be full of hard-working, salt-of-the-earth folks, each community doggedly proud of its own identity.

There were differences, of course. At home, the hillsides were currently encrusted in mud and ice while a Mediterranean climate ensured that the temperatures in Galilee rarely fell below freezing. Instead of slippery roads and snowstorms, here winter brought the rains that made the hillsides blossom with small wild red anemone (*Anemone coronaria*).

The lilies of the field? I wondered, inspecting the velvety red petals and black center. *The ones that don't toil and don't spin and don't worry about tomorrow but let tomorrow worry about itself?*

Scholars suggest that Jesus may have actually delivered these words, along with the rest of the Sermon on the Mount, in the hills west of the Sea of Galilee, closer to the first-century towns of Capernaum and Bethsaida. Still, the landscape where I sat was similar enough that I could picture farmers and fishermen, mothers and fathers, grandparents and grandchildren, leaving their work to gather at His feet. I could hear Him blessing them—the poor in spirit, the meek, the merciful. I could see Him stretching out His hand, motioning to the birds in the air and the flowers growing at their feet.

"Do not be anxious about your life . . ." Jesus tells them. "Look at the birds of the air . . . consider the lilies of the field."[4] It was all so peaceful. So serene. Exactly the kind of place you could leave your troubles and burdens. Exactly the kind of place you could escape the turmoil and pressures of life. Exactly the kind of place you could believe that peace—both internal and external—was possible.

---

4. Matthew 6:25–28.

Exactly the last place I expected to stumble across a Soviet anti-tank gun.

The large rusted-out weapon sat just yards from where I'd been considering the lilies of the field; the left wheel had broken off years ago, giving it a slightly cockeyed lean, but its turret still pointed faithfully down toward the towns surrounding the Sea of Galilee. My friends told me that the hillside where we sat had once been part of the disputed border between Israel and Syria. During the 1960s, Syrian guerillas, backed by the Soviet Union, had shelled the kibbutzim and towns at its base. Eventually Israel pushed Syria back past her own border and then annexed the land they had occupied. Years later, this particular area of the Golan was quiet enough for tourists and picnickers, even while the remnants of war still littered the hillsides.

Weapons of war surrounded by carefree wild red anemones.

The juxtaposition was startling at first, but the more I thought about it, the more it made sense. Galilee had always had its share of conflict, whether it was neighboring armies in the mid-twentieth century or invading Romans in the first. The people of those towns—Bethsaida, Chorazin, Capernaum—knew difficulty. But even in times of relative peace, they were real people. People who carried the burdens of relationships, work, family life, and personal frustration. People who knew stress. People who, like me, struggled to sleep at night.

As much as I wanted to create this idyllic vision of a place where I could escape the difficulties of the world, it simply wasn't possible. No place is immune to care or worry. No place untouched by the violence and burdens of this life. Seeing that antitank gun reminded me of this and put Jesus' call to consider the lilies into an entirely different perspective. *If Jesus isn't calling us to escape the cares of this world, what is He calling us to?*

The Peace of Wild Things

*"When despair for the world grows in me / and I wake
in the night at the least sound . . . I come into the peace
of wild things."* —Wendell Berry

As I lay awake at night thinking about all the things that I should
have done and all the things I shouldn't have done, I could never
escape the fact that most of them were trivial. An unreturned email,
forgetting to move the clothes from the washer to the dryer, the
conversation I kept putting off, the growing pile of invoices that
needed to be submitted. It felt ridiculous. Why do all these "little"
things amount to so much? Why do small burdens feel so heavy?

I wonder if I wasn't worrying about these little things themselves
so much as what these little things revealed about larger things—
about what they revealed about my larger helplessness. I shouldn't
have to worry about small things because I should be able to handle
small things. I *should* be able to return emails on time. I *should* be
able to sleep at night. *But if I can't handle little things, what can I
handle?* Failure at small things reminds us of how helpless we are
in this great, wide world. When little things spiral out of control,
they remind us that even they were never within our control in the
first place.

And this is terrifying.

Jesus understood this. He understood that small things can un-
settle us more than large things; so when He called the people of
Galilee to leave their anxiety—when He calls us to do the same—
He does so in context of very mundane, very ordinary concerns.

"Do not be anxious about your life," He assures them, "what
you will eat or what you will drink, nor about your body, what you
will put on."[5]

---

5. Matthew 6:25.

It's striking, really. Here, in the middle of arguably the greatest sermon ever, Jesus talks about our daily worries, whatever they may be. He talks about how we stress over food and clothing and how we obsess over our physical bodies. At the same time, He doesn't shame us for worrying about them. He doesn't tell us to just be grateful, to remember how much better we have it than other people. He doesn't tell us that we simply need to be more productive or to work harder. Instead, He asks whether our worry is actually accomplishing anything.

"And which of you by being anxious can add a single hour to his span of life? And why are you anxious about clothing?"[6]

Does fretting over meals and laundry produce more food or clean clothes? Does lying awake at night do anything to change situations that are completely outside your control in the first place? No. All your anxiety, all your worry, all your sleeplessness can't change a thing. And suddenly you come face to face with your limitations. Suddenly you realize how little you control your life. Suddenly you begin to understand why you feel like you're withering on the vine—why you feel so weak and wilting and unable to produce lasting fruit.

But Jesus doesn't leave it there. Instead, He draws our attention to the natural world, the birds of the air and the flowers of the field. He tells us to learn what they already know, to enter into "the peace of wild things." He calls us outside our current perception of reality to remember who *really* cares for us.

"But if God so clothes the grass of the field . . . will he not much more clothe you, O you of little faith?"[7]

We may be unable to cope with the most basic realities of existence; but He isn't. In fact, He's already providing food for the birds

6. Matthew 6:27–28.
7. Matthew 6:30.

and luxurious garments for the flowers. They don't worry because they know that their Creator cares for them. They don't worry because they know the One who keeps this world running.

And so, the bright red anemone can dance beside the gun's turret because she knows that the words of Isaiah the prophet ring true:

> Thus says God, the LORD,
>> who created the heavens and
>>> stretched them out,
>> who spread out the earth and what
>>> comes from it,
> who gives breath to the people on it
>> and spirit to those who walk in it:
> "I am the LORD; I have called you in
>> righteousness;
>> I will take you by the hand and
>>> keep you."[8]

When we believe that we are responsible for our own existence, when we trust our ability to care for ourselves, we will have nothing but stress because we are unequal to the task. You know this. Deep inside, you know your limits even as you fight against them. You know your helplessness even as you press forward by sheer determination. But at some point, the world becomes too much, and the largeness of life threatens to overwhelm you. And when it does, you must stop. And you must do what Jesus told His friends and followers to do on that flowered hillside overlooking the Sea of Galilee: "Seek first the kingdom of God and his righteousness, and all these things will be added to you."

---

8. Isaiah 42:5–6.

Your heavenly Father knows what you need. He knows your heart is troubled. He also knows, better than you do, that all these things are beyond you. And so, this is what you must do, all that you must do: You must seek Him. And let Him take care of the rest.

FIGURE 2

Forsythia, *Oleaceae forsythia*

Chapter 2

Breaking Ground

"Might I," quavered Mary, "might I have a bit of earth?"
"Earth!" he repeated. "What do you mean?"
"To plant seeds in—to make things grow—to see them
come alive." —Frances H. Burnett

There is a lovely road that leaves the city and wanders out to where shops and houses give way to pastures and barns. It rises and falls with the contours of the land and appears to forever head to the mountains in the distance. In the fog of early spring and late fall, you must creep along this road, easing around corners and over hills, always alert to an oncoming vehicle or white-tailed deer. After a snowstorm, it may or may not be passable. But if you follow this road far enough, you'll eventually come to a small brick church, flanked by a lively creek on one side and by a graveyard on the other.

Most Sunday mornings, you'll find me at this small brick church. If you come around ten o'clock, you may even find me with my knees wedged under a two-and-a-half-foot-high table, cutting and pasting the glories of the tabernacle onto sheets of colored construction paper. Other churches may have found it beneficial to halt such Sunday school programs, but we at Small Brick Church are stalwart believers in the power of Bible lessons, crafts, and snacks to lead little ones to God.

The results aren't immediately obvious, though. Like parents, Sunday school teachers must take the long view. We must accept that we will spend hours preparing a lesson, teach it with unmitigated enthusiasm, execute the perfectly themed craft—only to have the children return the following week having forgotten every last bit. Still, I've noticed something: Forgetting the story line doesn't stop children from raising their hands to answer questions. If there is anything they have learned, it's that "Jesus," "God," or "the Bible" is always a legitimate answer.

Children aren't the only ones to fall back on such truisms. Adults rely on similar answers when we face challenges. When life becomes overwhelming, when the questions hang in the air, it's easy to simply say "Jesus" or "the gospel." When a loved one is struggling through job loss or chronic illness, it's easy to simply say, "All things work together for good." And when you're facing burnout, it's easy to simply tell you to "Seek God."

But these answers are about as helpful as the answers I get from my four- and five-year olds. They are not wrong, but they are incomplete and imprecise. And if we're not careful, telling someone to "Seek God" without explaining how and what that looks like can actually compound her stress. Now, not only must she juggle day-to-day responsibilities, she must also figure out what it means to "Seek God." And when she tries and, for whatever reason, doesn't experience the rest she expects, she will feel more confused and more burdened. Apparently, not only is she incapable of finding time to cultivate her current relationships, she's also incapable of finding the largest Being in the universe.

So what does it mean to trust Jesus for rest? How does seeking His kingdom free us from anxiety and stress? He frees us from our burdens in the most unexpected way: He frees us by calling us to rely less on ourselves and more on Him. He frees us by calling us to humility.

Preparing the Soil

"When I first till at my place, the geese are flying north."
—Dick Raymond in *Joy of Gardening*

In the months after Jesus first invited His followers to leave their anxiety, He continued to teach and perform miracles in the broader region of Galilee. He formally called the twelve apostles away from their fishing nets and tax tables; and then He'd sent them out to teach and perform miracles themselves, without so much as a wallet, overnight bag, or by your leave. Eventually Jesus and His disciples reunite and find themselves near the place where He had first told them to consider the untroubled existence of the birds and the flowers.

And just as He had months before, He calls the crowds to leave their stress and promises them rest. "Come to me, all you who labor and are heavy laden," He says, "and I will give you rest." But this time, Jesus presses a bit further; His invitation intensifies: "Take my yoke upon you, and learn from me."[1] Again, Jesus directs their attention back to the natural world; but instead of pointing them to things that do not toil (like the birds or flowers), this time he points them to a beast of burden—the yoked ox.

Living in an agrarian society, even those who didn't work the fields would have understood the metaphor. The word "yoke" would have conjured up a picture of a farmer using an ox or donkey to prepare his field for planting. Before the first seeds and bulbs can enter the ground, a farmer must cultivate the soil to receive them. Left to itself, a field will quickly become overgrown with weeds, the soil will settle and harden, and changes in weather will make it rocky. Hardly a hospitable environment for tender roots and sprouts.

---

1. Matthew 11:28–29.

But plowing helps break up the soil and renew it.[2] After the harvest, a farmer will plow the leftover plant material under to decompose and enrich the soil before the next growing season. This plowing also turns up the grubs and pests living in the earth, making them easy prey for birds and rodents. Then, a few months later at the beginning of the growing season, another round of plowing aerates the soil, breaking the hard clods and redistributing the minerals. The goal is to produce soil that will drain well and be loose enough to let young roots push deep into the ground even as their sprouts push to the surface.

Today in the developed world, the work of plowing is done by tractors; and on our road, the work of plowing is done by Mr. Harold Dalton. Every spring and fall, Mr. Dalton plows the gardens of those of us who don't own a tractor. We don't always know when he'll come. It might happen after a chance meeting at the elementary school or an appointment made when our vehicles pass each other on the road and we both know to slow down and stop because it's getting to be that time of year. But at some point after we've harvested the last root vegetable, when the birds and squirrels have had sufficient opportunity to glean but before the ground freezes, I'll look out my kitchen window and see Mr. Dalton putting the soil to sleep for the winter. Then some morning, a few months later, when the forsythia (*Oleaceae forsythia*) is in bloom, heralding the coming spring, and the ground is workable, I'll look up and see Mr. Dalton waking it up again.

In lieu of a tractor or Mr. Harold Dalton, a farmer in the ancient world relied on his plow, a wooden yoke, and an ox to prepare his soil. The plow would have been made of wood and have

---

2. I'm using the term plowing here as inclusive of the more specific terms, plowing, disking, tilling, and harrowing, which designate different depths, types of attachments, and purposes for breaking ground.

a metal tip. A yoke, constructed of a wooden bar and rope, would connect the ox to the plow's shaft. As the ox pulled, the farmer would hold the plow handle with one hand, applying pressure to force the metal point into the ground; his other hand would prod the ox forward with a goad or stick. Farmers often waited for rain to soften the ground before attempting to plow, but even then, plowing was slow, plodding, deliberate work. Poet Marge Piercy describes the ox tethered to the plow as those of us "who strain in the mud and the muck to move things forward."[3]

So why would Jesus call people who were already burdened to shoulder another burden? Why would He believe plowing is a good image for rest?

Take My Yoke

"What does the LORD require of you, but to do justice, and to love kindness, and to walk humbly with your God?" —Micah 6:8

When you read the context of Jesus' words, you'll realize that Jesus isn't calling us to shoulder an extra burden; He is calling us to exchange a heavy burden for a lighter one. He is calling us to take *His* yoke because it is easier and lighter than the one we are presently carrying:

Take my yoke upon you, and learn from me, for I am gentle and lowly in heart, and you will find rest for your souls. For my yoke is easy, and my burden is light.

To understand the full extent of Jesus' invitation, you must also understand what the people were laboring under. What was the

---

3. Marge Piercy, "To be of use," in *Circles on the Water: Selected Poems of Marge Piercy* (New York: Knopf, 1982), 106.

source of their being "heavy laden" in the first place? What was the cause of their stress and anxiety?

Theologians note that this is not the only time that Jesus talks about the burdens we carry. In both their gospels, Luke and Matthew record Jesus condemning the religious leaders for weighing the people down with man-made laws and hypocritical judgments.

Woe to you lawyers also! For you load people with burdens hard to bear, and you yourselves do not touch the burdens with one of your fingers.[4]

and

The scribes and the Pharisees sit on Moses' seat . . . For they preach, but do not practice. They tie up heavy burdens, hard to bear, and lay them on people's shoulders, but they themselves are not willing to move them with their finger.[5]

One possible source of stress is the fact that we are submitted to unkind and unjust masters.[6] Some of us are hitched to the plow of men and women who happily abuse our spiritual sensitivity for their own benefit. These kinds of masters are not gentle and humble as Jesus is; they specialize in strict judgments and man-made rules that they themselves do not follow. So instead of being

---

4. Luke 11:46.
5. Matthew 23:2–4.
6. It is easy to confuse submission with humility. While Scripture teaches that all Christians submit to others within specific relationships (e.g., citizens to their government), the simple act of submitting does not ensure that we are either just or humble people. Because God is the ultimate source of authority, we submit to others only "as to the Lord." If an authority were to command us to act in violation of Christian teaching, it would be our righteous duty to refuse to submit. Simply following orders is no defense for sinful actions, whether it is within the church, home, or broader society.

motivated by goodness and beauty, we are driven forward by fear, threat of punishment, and manipulation. We feel the pressure to maintain picture-perfect lives and never step out of line lest we incur judgment. And we end up caught in a cycle of always evaluating our performance, always looking over our shoulder, always afraid and defensive.

In contrast, Jesus promises to be a kinder, gentler master. He promises that His yoke is easy and His burden is light. In John 3, He tells Nicodemus (a religious leader himself) that He did not come into the world to condemn the world but to save it.[7] And in his letter to the early churches in Galatia, the apostle Paul reiterates that "for freedom Christ has set us free . . . do not submit again to a *yoke* of slavery."[8] Unlike many of the religious leaders who sought power and personal glory, Jesus comes to bring us freedom and rest.

But this rest is contingent on something. We must come to Him. We must take His yoke. We must learn of Him. And here is the rub. Here is the real source of our anxiety and stress. Here is the root of our unhappiness: *The rest that Jesus offers only comes when we humble ourselves and submit to Him.*

This is why Jesus uses the image of a yoke; the yoke is a symbol of authority. By calling us to take *His* yoke, Jesus is calling us to submit to *Him* as our true master. But this can only happen when we "learn of Him"—when we are humbled as He is humble. Ironically, the heavy burden the people were struggling under, the thing that kept them from the rest, wasn't simply the weight

7. Do not miss the significance of Jesus telling Nicodemus that He did not condemn him. Here was a man caught in a system that evaluated his every move, teaching him that God's approval rested on his performance. He was so caught that the Scripture says that he came to Jesus "by night" ostensibly to avoid the scrutiny of his peers. But unlike the Pharisees, who specialized in condemnation, Jesus tells Nicodemus that He has come to deliver him from condemnation: "For God did not send his Son into the world to condemn the world," He assures him in John 3:17, "but in order that the world might be saved through him."
8. Galatians 5:1.

of other people's expectations. It was their belief that they had to meet those expectations by their own ability, leading to confidence that they could carry the burden alone. It was nothing other than pride and self-reliance. The same pride and self-reliance that keeps us from experiencing rest as well.

Messiah Complex

"Be not wise in your own eyes; fear the LORD*. . . .*
It will be healing to your flesh and refreshment
to your bones." —Proverbs 3:7–8

When I think about the stress in my life, I wouldn't initially associate it with pride. For me, the word "pride" conjures up an image of an arrogant, self-absorbed, loud-mouth bully. The swaggering pop star who courts fame and expects special treatment. The pushy queen bee who will do anything for the next promotion. The slick preacher who glad-hands his way to power and prestige. But that wasn't me. I was busy doing good things; I was trying to make a difference in the world.

And yet, my lack of peace was undeniable. My spirit was agitated, my mind restless, my emotions on edge. So when I'd read, "Come to me, all who labor and are heavy laden, and I will give you rest," I immediately identified. But when I read, "Take my yoke upon you, and learn from me, for I am gentle and lowly in heart," it didn't make as much sense. I recognized the symptoms; I just wasn't sure I agreed with the diagnosis. But being busy with good things didn't make me immune to pride. If anything, those of us who are busy "working for Jesus" may be the first to miss that we are struggling with pride because it can hide behind our good intentions. We can also miss it because we exist in contexts that excuse and, at times, actually encourage such self-reliance.

In her book *Unfinished Business*, Anne-Marie Slaughter shares her own crisis with stress and how the culture around her convinced her that she could (and should) "do it all." Slaughter is a former Princeton dean and president and CEO of the think tank New America, but for all her professional accomplishments, she's surprisingly honest about her struggles. Her own crisis came while working at the US State Department doing the good work of international diplomacy at the same time she was juggling family life as both a wife and mother.

"I had always believed, and told all the young women I taught and mentored, that women could 'have it all'," she writes. "They just had to be committed enough."[9]

The belief in her own competence drove Slaughter's daily choices. If she just worked hard enough, if she just had the right organizational system, if she just had enough support from the people around her, she could do it. But Slaughter confesses that this meant keeping a rigid schedule, spending time away from family, and regularly shortchanging her sleep. This left her

short-tempered and with a constant blurry feeling. . . . My schedule was often so finely calibrated that a kid's ear infection could send a week's worth of appointments toppling into one another like dominoes . . . even the most organized and most competent multitasker can reach her limit.[10]

It was coming face to face with her limits that eventually led Slaughter to resign her position at the State Department and scale back her schedule. But Slaughter doesn't view her decision to step

9. Anne-Marie Slaughter, *Unfinished Business: Women, Men, Work, Family* (New York: Random House, 2015), xvii.
10. Slaughter, 20, 68.

away as a failure; instead, she sees it as a symptom of a larger culture that holds inhumane and unrealistic expectations for our work.

But the marketplace isn't the only context that honors us when we push past normal human boundaries and encourages us to put confidence in ourselves; it happens in the home as well. No longer is it enough to have a good marriage; you must have the best one. No longer is it enough to feed, clothe, and protect your children from general harm; you must dress them on trend (preferably in clothes handmade from vintage fabric or knit from organic wool); make all their food from scratch (locally sourced, of course); and teach them to read by age four. And woe to you if you make the wrong choice of whether to breast or bottle-feed; whether to immunize or not; whether to send them to public or private school. Future generations depend on your decision, and we will not be held responsible if, and when, you make the wrong one.

The belief that "success" is within our grasp also invades our churches. If only you are committed enough, if only you are passionate enough, you are told, you can "do great things for God." At first, this message is inspiring. It taps into your God-given desire to work and do good. And so you push and press to "make your life count" only to see celebrity speakers and megachurch pastors take center stage at sold-out conferences while you slog away at a small brick church that sits at a bend in the road. And suddenly trying to change the world—and seeing it stay very much the same—feels like nothing other than the weight of the world resting on your shoulders.

And now you can see the relationship between pride and stress. Pride convinces us that we are stronger and more capable than we actually are. Pride convinces us that we must do and be more than we are able. And when we try, we find ourselves feeling "thin, sort of stretched . . . like butter that has been scraped over too much bread."[11] We begin to fall apart physically, emotionally, and spiritually for the simple reason that we are not existing as we were meant to exist.

Jesus' words are inescapable: "Come to me, all who labor and are heavy laden, and I will give you rest. Take my yoke upon you, and learn from me, for I am gentle and lowly in heart, and you will find rest for your souls."[12]

If you are not experiencing His rest, if you are weighed down, put out, and resentful, you must ask yourself whether you're actually pulling under His yoke. If you're feeling burdened and heavy laden, you must question whether you're as humbly submitted to Him as you believe yourself to be. You may have thrown off the yoke of religious form, you may be working for the greater good, but it's entirely possible that you are still plowing under your own direction and strength. Instead of embracing Jesus as your Messiah, it's entirely possible that you've become your own messiah.

It's entirely possible that you've begun to live beyond your means in a most literal sense.

So how would you know? What might signal that you have taken too much on yourself, that you are suffering under a "messiah complex"?

- Do you find yourself on a mission to save everyone and everything around you? Are you confused by which problems require your attention because they all seem to need it?
- Do you quickly take on new responsibilities because "somebody has to do it," but end up feeling overwhelmed and regretful that you took them on in the first place?
- Do you feel underappreciated and easily slip into self-pity?
- Do you find yourself irritated by people or struggling to

11. J. R. R. Tolkien, *The Fellowship of the Ring* (New York: Del Rey, 1986), 34.
12. Matthew 11:28–29.

forgive them when they fail? Do friends and family rarely meet your expectations?

- Do you work hard but never feel like it is enough?
- Do you find yourself tempted to escape daily pressure through the abuse of food, alcohol, social media, or pharmaceuticals?
- Do you regularly and consistently lack peace?

These questions are not exhaustive, nor are they intended to diagnose or shame. They are simply an opportunity for you to be uncomfortably honest with yourself. When we disregard our natural human limitations, we set ourselves in God's place. When we insist that our voice and our work is essential and must be honored, we set ourselves in God's place. When we believe that with enough effort, enough organization, or enough commitment, we can fix things that are broken, we set ourselves in God's place. And when we do, we reap stress, restlessness, and anxiety. Instead of submitting to His yoke, we break it and run wild, trampling the very ground we are meant to cultivate.

Humble Beasts

"People have forgotten this truth," the fox said. "But you mustn't forget it. You become responsible forever for what you've tamed." —Antoine de Saint-Exupéry

Out where the shops and houses give way to pastures and barns, a creek flows beside a small brick church and through an adjoining field. A wooden fence forms a boundary between the church property and the field; behind the fence, cows graze. Sometimes they lift their heads to watch the parishioners come and go from the weekly services, but they quickly lower them again, grasping mouthfuls of grass and grinding it methodically between their shifting jaws. In the summer, when the sun is high, they drift down to where the creek widens and the water pools under the shade of the chestnut oaks. There they stand knee-deep in the muddy water, sluggishly swishing their tails back and forth. Every so often, one of them will offer a low, gentle bellow, but for the most part, they are quiet and content. They are at peace.

When Jesus calls us to take His yoke, when He invites us to find rest through submission, He is not satisfying some warped need for power or His own sense of pride. He is calling us to safety. The safety that comes from belonging to Him. The safety that comes from being tamed.

In the book of Jeremiah, the prophet describes the people of Jerusalem as cattle who have "broken the yoke . . . burst the bonds."[13] They have refused to come under the care and correction of their kind Master and instead are wandering free. But in wandering away, they have exposed themselves to danger. Jeremiah writes: "Therefore a lion from the forest shall strike them down; a wolf from the desert shall devastate them." By leaving the yoke of their Master, they have become prey for the wild, unpredictable world around them.

It is understandable that we fear the yoke. We fear the loss of control. We fear surrender. But we must also understand that without the protection of a good master, we are not safe. From the manipulation of other masters. From the expectations of society. From ourselves.

And so we must respond to Jesus' call. We must come to Him. We must come to Him and learn of His gentleness and humility. We must come to Him to be tamed.

And when we are, He promises that we will find rest for our souls.

---

13. Jeremiah 5:5–6; see also the story of Nebuchadnezzar's pride in Daniel 4.

FIGURE 3

Wild grape, *Vitis rotundifolia*

Chapter 3

Returning to Our Roots

"Agriculture, the employment of our first parents in Eden,
the happiest we can follow." —Thomas Jefferson

The bell above the door jingle-jangled as a thin man in his eighties entered Dot's Hair Bo-tique off Main Street. Dot hadn't owned Dot's for nearly twenty years, but when the new proprietress assumed ownership, she'd decided it wasn't worth upsetting the customer base by changing the name. In fact, very little had changed, and to be honest, it didn't need to. The flecked linoleum was still serviceable, the dryers on the salon chairs worked, and the square building itself required little maintenance. There'd been the necessary updates, and occasionally the second chair was rented out to another stylist, but for the most part, Dot's had simply aged along with its clientele.

"C'mon in, Mr. Jefferson," the beautician called out in a distinctive mountain lilt. "I'll be with y' jus' soon as I finish this cut." She waved vaguely in my direction. I was sitting in the hydraulic chair next to the sink, with a tropically themed cape draped over me and my wet hair clipped to the top of my head, its ends splayed out like a rooster's comb. "This here's t' new preacher's wife."

The man nodded. "No hurry. I ken wait."

He shuffled over to a salon chair and eased himself onto its green vinyl seat. Once settled, he removed his cap and smoothed back the long, white wisps that had brought him in.

"M' boy dropt me off early 'cause he got some errands to run."

This was the cue to ask about how his children were and how his health was holding up. Good and can't complain. Eventually, between the snips of the scissors and the buzz of the overhead fluorescent lights, conversation drifted to where I'd come from and who my people were. I asked about his in return.

"You're kin to Thomas Jefferson, aren' y'?" the beautician interjected as she bent over to inspect her work. She pulled on two strands of my hair, comparing their lengths. Dissatisfied, she clicked her scissors.

"That's wut they tell me," the man answered. "'Course I din' know it 'til I were in grade school. Jus' sittin' at m' desk—guess I couldn't've been more than sev'n or eight—an' the teacher is learning us a history lessun an' all a sudden she points t' me an' says 'An' Frank is kin t' him.'"

He chuckled quietly. "I were as surprised as t' rest of 'em."

Garden of Delight

Mr. Jefferson's kin, Thomas, was born in Albemarle County, Virginia, about two hours northeast of where we sat in Dot's Hair Bo-tique. There the western mountains gradually descend into rolling hills to create a region known as the Piedmont. When European settlers first began migrating to the area in the early 1700s, they came in search of farmland and the opportunities that eluded them in the increasingly crowded coastal cities. One of the first settlers was a planter and surveyor named Peter Jefferson, the father of Thomas.

Most people know Thomas Jefferson as a man of letters, the

author of such landmark documents as the Declaration of Independence and the Statute for Virginia for Religious Freedom (the precursor to the US Bill of Rights). But at heart, Jefferson was a naturalist like his father before him. He was never happier than when planning and cultivating his five-thousand-acre plantation just outside Charlottesville.[1]

Jefferson's vision for Monticello began early, and by the time he was twenty-five, he had already begun leveling ground to construct the main house. Drawing on his classical education, Jefferson integrated architecture, landscape design, and botany to create a place of beauty and industry. Verdant lawns, bountiful orchards, brightly colored flowerbeds, and productive kitchen gardens flowed together seamlessly, joined by a network of well-worn dirt paths. He would spend the next fifty-eight years of his life—despite war, diplomatic missions, even a stint as the third president of the United States—longing for and developing his own corner of Eden.

While some farmers limited themselves to a handful of marketable crops like tobacco, Jefferson was always experimenting, trying to find which varieties grew best in the new world. He believed that "the greatest service which can be rendered any country is to add a useful plant to its culture."[2] And so, over the course of his life, he cultivated over five hundred fruits and vegetables, along with countless ornamentals. Seeds and slips from the continent became neighbors with the newly discovered varieties that Lewis and Clark brought back from the West.

---

1. I would be remiss to ignore the ingenuity and industry of the African Americans who comprised the majority of the Monticello community. Jefferson may have been the mastermind behind the plantation, but to quote the award-winning musical *Hamilton*, "We know who's really doing the planting."
2. Barbara B. Oberg and J. Jefferson Looney, eds., *The Papers of Thomas Jefferson Digital Edition* (Charlottesville: University of Virginia Press Rotunda, 2008), http://rotunda.upress.virginia.edu/founders/TSJN-01–32–02–0080.

In some sense, Jefferson's work at Monticello was as much an expression of his belief in the American experiment as it was of his love of nature. This was a brave, new world. There were few scientific records and no local extension office to consult. Every temperature he recorded, every seedling he planted, every new variety that graced his table was an opportunity to prove that America could rival the horticultural and epicurean delights of Europe.

But for all his accomplishments, there was one thing Jefferson never successfully cultivated: a vineyard.

During his years as a diplomat in France, Jefferson acquired a taste for European wines. He had toured the vineyards of the Rhine, Moselle, and Champagne Valleys; and when he eventually returned home, he was determined to make a Monticello wine—a wine that would carry the flavor and sensibility of his beloved Virginia. But a quick look at his cultivation records show that things did not go smoothly. Despite Jefferson's attempts to establish nearly twenty different varieties of grapes, none were successful. The repeated failure probably surprised him because several varieties of grapes did flourish in the eastern United States. The native fox grape (*Vitis labrusca*) and scuppernongs, a type of muscadine (*Vitis rotundifolia*), grew in abundance, although neither was suitable for the quality of wine that Jefferson wanted. But when he attempted to grow European varietals, they inevitably sickened and died.

Years later, scientists figured out why: phylloxera, a root louse.

Deep within the New World soil lives a nearly invisible insect that feeds on the roots of grapevines. While it is feeding, the phylloxera releases toxins that damage the vine's root structure, inhibiting it from absorbing water and nutrients from the soil. The wounds to the root also expose it to fungal and bacterial infections. But because native North American grapes are naturally resistant to the damage of the phylloxera, Jefferson had little way of knowing why his European grapes repeatedly failed. He had little way of knowing that the soil of his beloved Monticello—a soil that had been so productive for so many other things—was infested.

Root Issues

"If anyone would like to acquire humility, I can, I think, tell him the first step. The first step is to realise that one is proud." —C. S. Lewis

In many ways, Jefferson's struggle to cultivate a vineyard is similar to our struggle to cultivate humility. Most of us would probably agree that we "should" be more humble. We see it as a noble virtue. We may even be convinced that humility is essential to experiencing rest. Without it, we will continue to be agitated, anxious, and frustrated because our pride will lead us to live beyond natural limitations. But until we understand the extent to which pride infects our everyday choices, we will never be at peace.

One of the clearest examples of the extent of our pride is how quickly it infiltrates even our attempts to "be humble." When you encounter a person who—for whatever reason—is "trying" to be humble, you can spot it almost immediately. You may not be able to articulate why, but you know that the person is not actually humble. In fact, false modesty is so prevalent in our culture that we even have a term for it: the humble brag.

A humble brag is a statement that initially sounds humble because it uses certain words like "humble" or "thankful," but ultimately it draws attention back to the person making it:

- "So grateful to be trusted with shepherding this church." (Translation: "I hold a position of importance and people listen to me!")

- "I'm so humbled to see my art bless so many people."
  (Translation: "Look how many people read my books, come
  to my concerts, and listen to my lectures!")
- "What did I do to get such a hard-working, attractive,
  thoughtful man!?! For some reason, he loves me and treats
  me like a queen."
  (Translation: "A wonderful man loves me so I must be won-
  derful, too!")
- "My kid made the honor roll at XYZ Middle School."
  (Translation: "My kid is really smart—what can yours do?")
  and perhaps the most famous humble brag of all . . .
- "God, I thank you that I am not like other men."[3]
  (Translation: "I am better than other people.")

If we're honest, we've all let pride corrupt our attempts at humility. Of course, we all manifest it a bit differently. Some of us
debase ourselves or use self-deprecating language as a way to in-
vite reassurance and praise.[4] After a personal success, we may deflect well-wishes and congratulations, which simply forces those
around us to repeat them. And sometimes we will even wallow in
our "unworthiness" as a means of signaling our spiritual superiority; unlike other people, we are aware of our helplessness.

Part of the problem is that we misunderstand the nature of
both pride and humility. We tend to think of pride as something
we can conquer and of humility as something we can attain.
We know that we are supposed to model Jesus' own humility.
We know that God "opposes the proud"[5] and so we commit to

---

3. Luke 18:11.
4. As Mr. Darcy notes in Jane Austen's *Pride and Prejudice*: "Nothing is more deceitful
than the appearance of humility. It is often only carelessness of opinion and sometimes an
indirect boast."
5. James 4:6.

practicing humility, to intentionally "be humble." But humility is not a commodity. It is not something you can achieve. It is not something you earn or accomplish. Being humble is something you either *are* or you *aren't*. And if you aren't, no amount of trying can make up for it. All your attempts to "be humble"—to say the right words or deflect praise or carry yourself in a lowly way—will seem unnatural and put on.

In a sense, humility follows the classic writing adage: "Show, don't tell." In order for a story to be believable, authors use actions and dialogue to *show* a character's nature instead of simply *telling* you about him. For example, if I write a novel and introduce you to a character with the line "Philip was a humble man," it will fall flat. You may accept it out of courtesy, but you would not be convinced that Philip is a humble man because you haven't yet seen him act in `a humble way. At best, he would seem one-dimensional; at worst, phony. But what if I introduce Philip to you this way:

> Philip rolled up his sleeves and knelt beside the old man. As the freshly turned earth soaked into his woolen trousers, he thought about what Mrs. Pickering had said last time he'd come home with muddy knees:
>
> "A Reverend Doctor shouldn't be down in the dirt planting an old man's geraniums, even if that man does have rheumatoid arthritis."

Read this paragraph and you will immediately *know* that Philip is a humble person. You will also know that Mrs. Pickering isn't. Why? Because their actions and words reveal their character. Despite his education and status in the community, Philip is down in the dirt helping a feeble old man. Despite the old man's handicap, Mrs. Pickering doesn't believe Philip should lower himself.

The same is true of humility. If a person must announce his

humility because we wouldn't see it otherwise, he is not a truly humble person. Just as an author gradually reveals the nature of her characters, our words and actions gradually reveal our character and our essential nature. If we are humble people, it will be obvious. But if we are proud people, this will be abundantly obvious as well. Jesus Himself teaches this principle in Luke 6:45 when He says,

> The good person out of the good treasure of his heart produces good, and the evil person out of his evil treasure produces evil, for out of the abundance of the heart his mouth speaks.

So when Jesus calls us to learn of His own humility, He's not calling us to adopt humble posturing or master a new skill. He intends to fundamentally change us. He intends to strip us of the pride that keeps us from experiencing rest. He intends to get to the root of the problem so that humility becomes natural to us.

Blight

"Pride is the deepest root of the malignancy within ourselves."
—Dietrich von Hildebrand

Thomas Jefferson wasn't the only grower to struggle with the effects of the phylloxera. During the mid-1800s, French winemakers came close to losing their entire industry due to this microscopic pest. Some time during the late 1850s, phylloxera, which is native to North America, was carried across the Atlantic causing what historians call the Great French Wine Blight.[6] Initially growers didn't know what was happening; an "unknown disease" (or as

---

6. Pat Montague, "The Great French Wine Blight," *Wine Tidings* 96, July/August 1986, www.wampumkeeper.com/wineblight.html.

the French called it, *la nouvelle maladie de la vigne*) was attacking their vines. One or two vines would flag; the leaves would become discolored, turning yellow and eventually red; and then they would dry up and fall off. The following season, the same symptoms would spread to nearby vines. Even if the vines could produce fruit, it would be acidic and watery. By the third season, the vines would be dead with no apparent cause.

Growers tried everything from chemical pesticides to using hens to eat insects off the vines. But the blight spread quickly, devastating the very vineyards that had inspired Jefferson. Over the course of fifteen years, phylloxera killed nearly 40 percent of French vines and threatened the entire European wine industry. The most infuriating part was that scientists could see the effects of the blight—the withering, the discoloration, the lack of fruit—but they couldn't pinpoint the cause because the damage was happening at the root source. When growers excavated the roots of dead vines, they found them black and decomposed, but they didn't notice the phylloxera because they had already moved on to feed on healthy roots. A breakthrough finally came when scientists observed that dying, although not yet dead, vines had the insects clinging to their roots. But even then there was debate. Many insisted that the phylloxera were parasites simply taking advantage of weakened vines; they were an effect of the blight, not the cause itself.

But vines continued to die, and the blight spread.

Like these French vintners, we can often see the effects of pride and how it contributes to our overall lack of peace. We may agree that the infestation is so profound that it corrupts even our attempts at humility. But like them, we often mistake our emotional unsettledness as simply taking advantage of our difficult circumstances. As a result, we justify our short tempers and agitation because we're "under stress." We convince ourselves that our worry is normal because we have so much responsibility. And we end up treating the symptoms instead of the root cause.

When we feel overwhelmed, we establish stricter boundaries and coach ourselves to say no more often. When we are tired, we trust a vacation or carving out "me-time" to alleviate our stress. When we find ourselves falling behind in our work, we commit to better scheduling and longer days. When we feel like we can never do enough, we tell ourselves to just "embrace the mess." And while any of these could be potentially helpful—having poultry eat insects off plants did offer some benefit—none of them resolve the root issue. None of them eradicate the pride that is feasting on our souls.

If we establish strict boundaries without accepting our lack of control, we'll simply be harried and unhappy in a smaller space. If we go on vacations without cultivating humility, we'll return to our stress once the bags are unpacked. If we schedule every available minute without acknowledging our own temporariness, we'll become a slave to the calendar. And if we try to "embrace the mess" without understanding where the mess came from in the first place, we'll never grow past it.

As long as we refuse to accept that our pride is the source of our unrest, we will continue to wither on the vine.

Humble Roots

"Humility, that low, sweet root / From which all heavenly virtues shoot." —Thomas Moore

Part of the reason French growers struggled to accept that the phylloxera was causing the blight was because doing so threatened their own sense of identity. Wine making is a tradition steeped in history, local culture, and a strong sense of place. Wines, like many types of cheese, are associated with the region they come from; and everything about that place—the specific soil, the yearly weather patterns, the unique variety of grape that flourishes there—all this goes into the bottle. Champagne is not simply a fancy name for a sparkling wine; it is a wine produced with pride in the Champagne region of France.

If phylloxera was the cause of the blight, then growers only had one option: a radical solution known as "reconstitution." In order to save their vineyards, some of which had been passed down through generations, they'd have to graft their healthy vines onto North American rootstock that was immune to the attack of phylloxera. The vines would retain their individual identity, but the roots would be foreign. To some growers, this suggestion was a greater offense than the blight itself. In their pride, they convinced themselves of the sufficiency of their own roots and continued to use insecticides and other treatments to fight the symptoms. But the vines continued to die.

And suddenly we begin to understand what's at stake in our fight against pride. What's at stake is our own sense of identity.

In John 15, hours before Jesus surrenders Himself to the cross, He tells His disciples that in order to bear fruit, they must "abide in him."

I am the true vine, and my Father is the vinedresser. . . . Abide in me, and I in you. As the branch cannot bear fruit by itself, unless it abides in the vine, neither can you, unless you abide in me. I am the vine; you are the branches. Whoever abides in me and I in him, he it is that bears much fruit, for apart from me you can do nothing.[7]

---

7. John 15:1, 4–5.

Here is the offense: "Apart from me, you can do nothing." Apart from Jesus, our leaves will turn yellow and fall off. Apart from Jesus, the fruit we bear will be watery and acidic, unfit for anything. Apart from Jesus, we will wither up and die.

Just as the French growers had to choose between holding on to their pride and saving their vineyards, we must also choose. The problem, at this point, isn't that we can't see the symptoms or even that we don't know what's causing our lack of peace. The problem is our unwillingness to accept the solution. The problem is our obsession with ourselves. With *our* need to fix things, *our* need to make ourselves better, *our* need to be approved by God and others, *our* need to "count for something."

But this is also why Jesus calls us to come to Him. By coming to Jesus, we remember who we are and who we are not. By coming to Him, we come face to face with God and with ourselves. "It is only in our encounter with a personal God," writes philosopher Dietrich von Hildebrand, "that we become fully aware of our condition as creatures, and fling from us the last particle of self-glory."[8]

Humility, then, is not simply a disposition or set of phrases. Humility is accurately understanding ourselves and our place in the world. Humility is knowing where we came from and who our people are. Humility is understanding that without God we are nothing. Without His care, without His provision, without His love, we would still be dust. Or as nineteenth-century pastor Andrew Murray writes in his classic book *Humility*, "Humility is simply acknowledging the truth of [our] position as creature and yielding to God His place."

But this is also why it's so difficult to come to Jesus for rest.

---

8. Dietrich von Hildebrand, *Humility: Wellspring of Virtue* (Manchester, NH: Sophia Institute Press, 1997), 24.

Before we can be grafted onto Him, we must be stripped of our decomposing roots, our self-sufficiency and ego. We must give up the pretense that we can root ourselves. We must reject the pride that believes in humility as a concept but refuses to actually be humbled before God. The trouble, of course, is that it is our very pride that keeps us from being healed of our . . . pride. So before we can even begin to answer His call to come to Him, Jesus comes to us. Because we could never sufficiently humble ourselves, Jesus humbles Himself. And by doing so, He became both the model and the means of our own humility. Through His life, death, and resurrection, Jesus shows us our true identity as people dependent on God for life. And through His life, death, and resurrection, He imparts this humble life to us once again.

Rooted in Christ

"The life of God is the root in which we are to stand and grow."
—Andrew Murray

In the 1980s—nearly two hundred years after Jefferson first tried—scientists and growers finally achieved his dream of a vineyard that could produce a Monticello wine. And they did it the same way scientists and growers eventually saved the French wine industry—by grafting European cuttings onto North American rootstock that was resistant to phylloxera.

We too must be grafted. If we are to find rest from our stress, if we are to have any hope of escaping our pride, we must be grafted onto the one who is humility Himself. We can no longer simply be content to attempt to imitate Him; we must become part of Him in order to reflect Him.

And this begins by remembering the truth about who we and where we come from. Like old Mr. Jefferson in Dot's Hair Bo-tique, we must learn about our roots. And we learn this by encountering Jesus Himself. Through His humanity, we learn what ours is supposed to be. Through His deity, He enables us to be what we are supposed to be. And when we are, when we exist as God has intended us to exist, we will find rest.

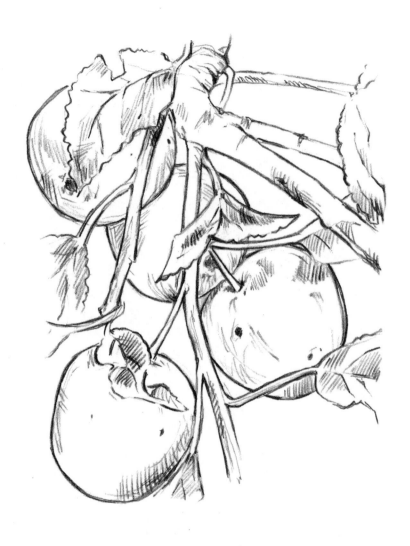

FIGURE 4

Domestic apple, *Malus domestica*

Chapter 4

Family Tree

*"I chanced / A goodly tree far distant to behold / Loaden
with fruit of fairest colours mixed / Ruddy and gold."*
—John Milton

When a three-and-half-foot long, six-inch-wide package
landed on my doorstep one afternoon, I didn't think
much of it. I hadn't ordered anything that fit those proportions,
but Nathan regularly has packages shipped to the house instead
of the church. When I took the box inside, though, I realized that
the package wasn't for the church after all. The return label read:

> David C. Vernon
> Century Farm Orchards
> Reidsville, NC

Still, this didn't surprise me either; Nathan also regularly orders from seed and plant catalogs. When we bought our home
a few years ago, the land around it was largely uncultivated, a
blank canvas for his imagination. Within weeks, he'd begun planting—hedgerows, berry bushes, an asparagus bed. He even ripped
out the holly bushes in the front yard (because "I don't like holly

bushes") and replaced them with a garden of ornamentals: daffodils, bleeding hearts, a butterfly bush, boxwoods, and hydrangea.

Within a few hours, Nathan came home and his eyes lit up as soon as he saw the box.

"Oh, good. They're here!"

"They?"

Too excited to bother answering me, he lifted the box onto the kitchen table and grabbed his penknife from his back pocket. A few quick slits and the box sprang open. He reached in and rustled through the paper and plastic packaging. Then he removed what I could only assume were five dead sticks. His face beamed.

"These are the apple trees I ordered."

I leaned in for a closer look. The "trees" were just slips, thin as my pinky finger, about three feet long, and bare-rooted. They looked more like the beginning of a wicker basket than the beginning of an orchard. I looked at Nathan, back at the sticks, and then back to Nathan.

"Those are trees?"

"What else would they be? I'm going to plant them along the southern edge of the garden, along the property line." He began laying them out on the table, reading the white handwritten tag attached to each one. "Johnson Keeper. William's Favorite. Esopus Spitzenburg—this was one of Thomas Jefferson's favorites —Yellow June. And Mary Reid."

He looked up at me like a puppy that had just dropped a ball at my feet.

"They're heirloom varieties. They're from this orchard in North Carolina that specializes in old southern apples." He fingered the one labeled Yellow June. "I got this one because it's a good pollinator. And this one—the Johnson Keeper—ripens late in October and is supposed to store well through the winter."

He continued to tell me his plans for these sticks: how they'd come into fruit at different points of the season, how he'd protect them from deer and rodents, how he wanted to preserve local agricultural heritage. Only half listening, I peered over the edge of the box and saw a white piece of paper shoved to one corner. It was the invoice. I pulled it out and flattened it. Sure enough, there they were. Each stick carefully inventoried and priced at twenty-five bucks a pop.

To be fair, Nathan's interest in heirloom[1] apples is more than an indulgence. He's always wanted to grow fruit trees, and by selecting heirloom varieties, he is doubling his efforts. Not only is he cultivating usable fruit, he's become part of a broader conservation movement. As food production moved from backyards and family farms to large-scale industrial enterprises, particular apples were cultivated for their resistance to disease and long shelf life. This increased corporate efficiency but reduced biodiversity. During the mid-1800s, thousands of apple varieties existed; today the market is dominated by a couple dozen. Your average grocery store carries the common ones—Fuji, Granny Smith, Yellow and Red Delicious, McIntosh, and Honeycrisp. But to enjoy a Yellow Transparent or a Winesap, you'll have to hunt along the edges of homesteads and talk to the old-timers. If that doesn't work, you'll have to order them from Century Farm Orchards for twenty-five dollars apiece and grow them yourself.

One of the challenges to propagating heirloom apples, though, is that you can't simply plant a new tree from a seed. In order to produce fruit, apple trees must be pollinated, but because trees usually cross pollinate—the pollen from a Yellow June pollinates the flower of a Mary Reid—the resulting fruit will be a Mary Reid

---

1. Some conservationists differentiate between the words "heirloom" (used for plants) and "heritage" (used for animals). I've seen them used interchangeably in my research, but for purposes of this book, I'm adhering to the difference.

apple, but the seeds inside it will produce an entirely different variety in the next generation. Put that seed into the ground, and you'll get a cross between a Yellow June and Mary Reid, with no guarantee of which genetic information will dominate.

So when growers want to preserve a certain variety of apple, they must cut a scion (a twig or shoot with buds) from the original tree and graft it onto rootstock. But unlike French wine growers who grafted to protect against disease, apple growers graft to preserve a particular genetic composition. As food writer Rowan Jacobsen explains, "Every McIntosh is a graft of the original tree that John McIntosh discovered on his Ontario farm in 1811, or a graft of a graft. Every Granny Smith stems from the chance seedling spotted by Maria Ann Smith in her Australian compost pile in the mid-1800s."[2] And if you go back far enough you'll end up in a garden in central Asia around 2000 BC, where the very first domestic apple tree (*Malus domestica*) was cultivated.

First Fruits

"It is remarkable how closely the history of the apple tree is connected with that of man." —Henry David Thoreau, Wild Apples

Like cultivating heirloom apples, cultivating humility is an exercise in family history and genetic lines. In many ways, cultivating humility is about recovering a variety of human identity that nearly went extinct. And like the first domestic apple tree, it all starts in a garden in central Asia.

In the last chapter, I defined humility as a correct sense of self,

---

2. Rowan Jacobsen, "Why Your Supermarket Sells Only 5 Kinds of Apples," *Mother Jones*, Mar/Apr 2013, http://www.motherjones.com/environment/2013/04/heritage-apples-john-bunker-maine.

as understanding where you come from and where you belong in this world. This definition becomes clearer when you remember how the Scripture describes human origins. Genesis 1 tells us that human beings are made in the image of God, destined to reflect and represent Him on the earth:

> Then God said, "Let us make [mankind]³ in our image, after our likeness. And let them have dominion over . . . all the earth and over every creeping thing that creeps on the earth." So God created man in his own image, in the image of God he created him; male and female he created them.⁴

But Genesis 2 adds another layer to our understanding of what it means to be human by telling us *how* God created mankind:

> Then the LORD God formed man of dust from the ground and breathed into his nostrils the breath of life, and the man became a living creature. And the LORD God planted a garden in Eden, in the east, and there he put the man whom he had formed.⁵

Fascinatingly, while humans were made to rule over the earth, we were also made *from* the earth. And perhaps even more significantly, we only came alive by God's Spirit. Without God's breath in us, we are nothing but a pile of dirt.

This earthy imagery repeats itself throughout the Scripture. In Psalm 103, David sings that God shows compassion on us, in part, because "He remembers that we are dust."⁶ The prophet Jeremiah

---

3. The Hebrew word is *adam* which here refers to "mankind" and only later in the text is used as a proper noun to designate the first male, Adam.
4. Genesis 1:26–27.
5. Genesis 2:7–8.
6. Psalm 103:14.

likens humans to a lump of clay on the potter's wheel, being shaped and formed by the sovereign hands of the Potter.[7] In the parable of the sower, Jesus compares the human heart to different types of soil that either receive or reject God's word. And in his second letter to the Corinthians, Paul reminds them that we are simply "jars of clay, to show that the surpassing power belongs to God and not to us."[8]

Even more interestingly, the English words "human" and "humility" share a common Latin root: *humus*, which means dirt, earth, or ground. (Gardeners will quickly recognize the English transliteration, humus, which itself refers to a particular type of nutrient-rich soil.) Ancient Hebrew reveals a similar linguistic pattern. In the Genesis narrative, the word *adam* is a collective noun meaning "humankind" and comes from the Hebrew word *adamah* which means "ground." Linguistically, at least, there is an intrinsic connection between the ground, our humanity, and humility.

In other words, humility begins by remembering where we come from. Humility begins by remembering that to be human is to be dirt. Humility begins by remembering that we are "dust and to dust [we] shall return."[9]

The link between our humanity and humility also helps us understand what happens at another crucial point in our spiritual genetic history. After creating the man and woman, God tasks them with caring for each other and cultivating the world; as the text puts it, they are to be "fruitful and multiply" and "have dominion."[10] Dependent on their Creator for life, they are also to

---

7. Jeremiah 18:1–6.
8. 2 Corinthians 4:7.
9. Genesis 3:19.
10. Genesis 1:28.

live dependently on each other as partners in that life.[11]

As part of their commissioning, God also cordons off the tree of the knowledge of good and evil. The man and woman could eat of every other tree in the garden, but they could not eat of this one. This was the boundary between the creature and the Creator. Only the Creator God had a right to access this tree. Only He had the right to know (or establish) good and evil. To consume the tree of the knowledge of good and evil would be, in essence, to reject God as God and establish mankind in His place. To consume the tree of the knowledge of good and evil would be to deny everything that is true of the creature's dependence on God. To consume the tree of the knowledge of good and evil would be to deny our own humanity.

Forbidden Fruit

Over the centuries, Christian artists have often represented the tree of the knowledge of good and evil as an apple tree. Historians aren't exactly sure why this is the case—artists could have as easily chosen a fruit like an apricot or pomegranate—but to this day, even at the small brick church at the bend in the road, an apple tree it is. When I teach my fours and fives the creation story, our coloring page invariably includes a cartoonish tree with large, unnaturally red apples hanging from its boughs. Regardless of who first depicted the forbidden fruit as an apple, the association was probably most permanently (and masterfully) reinforced in John Milton's *Paradise Lost*. In Book Nine, Milton opens the serpent's

---

11. God's statement in Genesis 2:18 that "It is not good that the man should be alone" should not be construed to mean that only those in marriage or romantic relationships are experiencing their full human potential. Male and female are mutually dependent on each other throughout all spheres of human existence, not simply in our reproductive capacities. Mutual dependence certainly includes sexuality, but is not limited to it, if only because the Trinity reveals a similar mutual dependence and communion.

temptation of the woman with this description of the tree and its fruit. Here, the serpent speaks:

> I chanced
> A goodly tree far distant to behold,
> Loaden with fruit of fairest colours mixed,
> Ruddy and gold. In nearer drew to gaze;
> When from the boughs a savoury odour blown
>
> . . .
>
> To satisfy the sharp desire I had
> Of tasting those fair Apples, I resolved
> Not to defer; hunger and thirst at once,
> Powerful persuaders, quickened at the scent
> Of that alluring fruit, urged me so keen.
> About the mossy trunk I wound me soon;
> For, high from ground, the branches would require
> Thy utmost reach, or Adam's; round the Tree
> All other beasts that saw, with like desire
> Longing and envying stood, but could not reach.

It's significant that Milton portrays the forbidden fruit (apple or not) as growing "high from the ground" and that the serpent climbed the tree to reach it. As the serpent explains to the woman, "the branches would require / Thy utmost reach, or Adam's." In order to consume the fruit, the woman and man would have to move away from the ground from which they had been formed. In order to consume the fruit, they would have to lift themselves up.

This lifting up, this pride, is central to the scriptural narrative as well. In Genesis 3, the serpent does not immediately tempt the woman with the fruit (although the woman does recognize it as "a delight to the eyes"). Instead the serpent begins by suggesting that God is protecting His pride at the expense of hers. "God knows," the serpent hisses, "that when you eat of it your eyes will be opened, and you will be like God, knowing good and evil."[12] This suggestion, of course, is the product of the serpent's own pride, which Isaiah describes this way: "You said in your heart, 'I will ascend to heaven; above the stars of God I will set my throne on high. . . . I will make myself like the Most High.'"[13]

Ego. That's what's at stake here. Nothing short of the need to believe ourselves more important than we actually are. Nothing short of the need to lift ourselves up. The rooster puffing out his feathers to appear bigger than he is. The lap dog barking loudly to convince himself he's the leader of the pack. The gorilla beating his chest to assert his dominance.

And so often ego is at the root of our present unrest, as well.

We run ourselves ragged trying to keep up with the Joneses to prove to ourselves that we are as important as we think we are. We see friends achieving success, maybe even in ministry, and rather than rejoicing with them, we somehow feel smaller. So we privately tally our spiritual "successes," reassuring ourselves that we're just as necessary as they are. Or perhaps one morning you're scrolling through your social media feed, when you see her—the woman you secretly compare yourself with—and she's just posted pictures of her latest family trip (to a place you could never afford). There she sits, effortlessly beautiful even with vacation hair, her arms wrapped around her spunky, albeit well-behaved, children, her adoring husband standing next to her, smiling. And suddenly the rest of the day is ruined for you.

Why? Why can another person's success disturb you so deeply?

---

12. Genesis 3:5.
13. Isaiah 14:13–14.

Why do her vacation pictures make *your* life seem less important, smaller even? To riff off G. K. Chesterton, perhaps the reason your life seems smaller is because you've simply grown too big in it.[14]

At its root, pride confuses our identity with God's and makes us think of ourselves as larger than we really are. But when we begin to think of ourselves this way, we expect other people to think of us like this too. Without realizing it, we begin to expect more glory and more honor because we actually believe ourselves to be better than they are. So when normal everyday occurrences—like scrolling through Facebook—remind us that we aren't, our ego takes a hit. As pastor and theologian Tim Keller explains in his book *The Freedom of Self-Forgetfulness*, "the ego is fragile. That is because anything that is overinflated is in imminent danger of being deflated—like an overinflated balloon."[15]

Our need to maintain our overinflated sense of self is also why theologians mark pride as the root of every other sin; not only does pride go before the fall, it goes before every fall.[16] We covet because we believe that we deserve what other people have. We boast to remind others how important we are. We fight to prove ourselves stronger and more righteous. And so the exhausting game of comparison and competition cycles on and on and on. As C. S. Lewis writes, "Pride gets no pleasure out of having some-

---

14. In his essay "The Maniac," Chesterton asks, "But how much happier you would be if you only knew that these people cared nothing about you! How much larger your life would be if your self could become smaller in it; if you could really look at other men with common curiosity and pleasure."
15. Timothy Keller, *The Freedom of Self-Forgetfulness: The Path to True Christian Joy* (Chorley, England: 10Publishing, 2012), 20.
16. It is important to understand the connection between pride and our sinful actions. The danger for many of us is that we evaluate the state of our hearts based on whether we are *intentionally* sinning. The problem, of course, is that pride literally blinds us to the state of our own hearts; we will feel entirely justified in our choices. When this happens, we can convince ourselves that we are humble people, despite sin in our lives. Because of this, we must be quick to receive the reproof of trusted friends; they often see things that we simply cannot.

thing, only out of having more of it than the next man. . . . It is the comparison that makes you proud: the pleasure of being above the rest."[17]

So when something happens that punctures our sense of self—when we see someone with more than we have or who is more successful than we are—our ego begins to deflate. We feel smaller, not because we are smaller than other people, but because we had been thinking of ourselves "more highly than [we] ought."[18] We have lifted ourselves up; and as the most basic laws of physics demand, what goes up must come down.

Given our own struggle with pride, it's not surprising what eventually happens in the garden. The serpent appeals to the woman's ego, and all too quickly, she believes him. She and her husband consume the lie and it becomes part of them. And suddenly they become competitors instead of collaborators, their work an endless exercise in striving to prove their worth. When the creature postures itself as the Creator, humility goes all but extinct.

The Old Apple Tree

Here's to thee, old apple-tree,
Whence thou mayst bud, and whence thou mayst blow,
And whence thou mayst bear apples enow!
—Nineteenth-century English wassailing rhyme

For many conservationists, the desire to cultivate heirloom apples isn't simply to enjoy unusual varieties; they are working to preserve them from extinction. As backyard orchards and family farms have morphed into subdivisions and shopping malls, many

---

17. C. S. Lewis, *Mere Christianity: Comprising The Case for Christianity, Christian Behaviour, and Beyond Personality* (New York: Touchstone, 1996), 110.
18. Romans 12:3.

apple trees were either cut down or neglected to the point where disease and age overcame them. Others may still grow in thickets and along the edges of fields and homesteads, but we simply don't know where or what they are. Trees that once produced apples for sauces, pies, brandy, cider, and vinegar are literally lost to us, along with their unique genetic strains.

But one way conservationists can locate "lost" trees is by listening to rumors. They develop relationships with older folks and probe what apple searcher Tom Brown calls their "apple memories."[19] (Brown, who searches for heirloom apple trees in the Piedmont of western North Carolina, first became interested in them when he heard folks talking about a Harper's Seedling, a variety he'd never seen or tasted.) When Brown hears a rumor about a certain variety, he'll go out looking for it. Sometimes he goes house to house asking questions and using a network of informal channels—neighbors who remember an apple of that description down at the Quesenberry place; aged farmers whose cows graze under the boughs of trees planted by their granddaddies; ministers, who might not know about apples themselves, but who know the people who know. And when Brown finally identifies a tree, he takes a cutting to preserve that variety for future generations.

Since the fall, there have always been rumors that humility would be recovered, that human beings could once again taste its ripe fruit and live as we were intended to live. The first whispers came when God promised that the seed of the woman would crush the serpent who had tempted her. But the rumors echo through the rest of Scripture as well—a rumor of a tree that flourishes beside streams of water and produces good fruit;[20] a rumor of a healthy branch, a scion, which will generate from the tree of

19. Tom Brown, "The Search for Rare, Heritage Apples," *Mother Earth News*, February 1, 2013, http://www.motherearthnews.com/real-food/rare-heritage-apples-zb01302zrob.aspx.
20. Psalm 1:3.

David;[21] a rumor of a tender plant that has the potential to flourish in dry ground.[22]

But one of the most promising rumors is the one about the shoot that springs up out of a dead tree and bears fruit. To put it in the language of heirloom apples, folks remember a tree that had once flourished and produced abundant sweet fruit—fruit so large you'd have to hold it with two hands. And crisp and juicy, too. But the tree contracted a horrible disease and was cut down. They thought it was lost forever, and every time they walked past the stump, they remembered their loss. But then years later, out of nowhere, a shoot sprouted. A scion with buds. A glimmer of life. Isaiah tells it this way:

> There shall come forth a shoot from the stump of Jesse, and a
> branch from his roots shall bear fruit. And the Spirit of the LORD
> shall rest upon him,
> the Spirit of wisdom and understanding,
> the Spirit of counsel and might,
> the Spirit of knowledge and the fear of the LORD. And his delight
> shall be in the fear of the LORD. . . . In that day the root of Jesse,
> who shall stand as a signal for the peoples—of him shall the
> nations inquire, and his resting place shall be glorious.[23]

And now we come full-circle; now we see the whole picture. Jesus Christ is the one true Branch, the lost variety. Jesus Christ is the one who alone fears the Lord and who bears good fruit.

---

21. Jeremiah 23:5. Interestingly, the term "scion" has two meanings. The first is botanical: a shoot or branch from a tree that has buds that promise future growth. This is what apple searchers are looking for—they want to find a tree with enough life left in it to harvest a scion. The second use describes a descendent of a notable family—the heir that can continue the dynasty.

22. Isaiah 53:2.

23. Isaiah 11:1–3, 10.

Jesus Christ is the one who restores both our humility and our humanity. And in His glorious resting place—under the shade of His branches—we find rest.

In the Likeness of Men

"He became what we are so that he might make us what he is." —Athanasius of Alexandria

Perhaps no other passage of Scripture reveals Jesus' humility as much as Philippians 2:3–11 does. In writing to the early believers, the apostle Paul appeals to them not to be motivated by "selfish ambition or conceit, but in humility count others more significant than yourselves." In essence, don't let your overinflated ego control your choices. And to show them what this would look like, he tells them to have the "mind" of Christ Jesus, to learn of Him who is gentle and lowly in heart:

- Instead of believing that He had to fight to prove His worth, Jesus, *"though he was in the form of God, did not count equality with God a thing to be grasped."*
- Instead of trying to fulfill Himself, Jesus *"emptied himself."*
- Instead of working for His own comfort and glory, Jesus took *"the form of a servant."*
- Instead of throwing off and ignoring human limitations, Jesus was *"born in the likeness of men."*
- Instead of refusing to obey, insisting that He would not be told what to do, Jesus *"humbled himself by becoming obedient to the point of death."*

What Paul is describing is not simply a checklist of good human behaviors. Something about Jesus' very existence—about the way He moved through the world as a human being—radically altered humanity. Just as the choices of the first man and woman affected generations to come, so the choices of Jesus affected generations to come.[24] This is the mystery and the hope of the incarnation: We are restored as much by the life of Christ as by His death and resurrection. In *The Jesus We Missed*, Patrick Henry Reardon writes,

> The doctrine of the Incarnation affirms that we were redeemed through the personal experiences of God's Son in human history—the very things that the Word underwent. . . . Human redemption 'happened' in the humanity of the eternal Word as he passed through, transformed, and deified our existence.[25]

Jesus' humanity restores our humanity. Jesus' humility restores our humility.

The temptation, of course, is to bypass Jesus altogether. The temptation is to read these verses as a model for our behavior and then attempt to live them out in our own strength. We believe Jesus to be the perfect humanity and even see His humility as the ideal. But then we strive for the ideal apart from Him. We insert ourselves in the narrative as if we were Jesus. We talk about being "Jesus' hands and feet" and then proceed to act independently of Him. We ask, "What would Jesus do?" but really mean, "What would Jesus do if He were me?"

We forget that without the Breath of Life in us, we are nothing but dirt.

The core issue, and the theme of this book, is this: We are not

---

24. 1 Corinthians 15:22.
25. Patrick Henry Reardon, *The Jesus We Missed: The Surprising Truth about the Humanity of Christ* (Nashville: Thomas Nelson, 2012), 27.

Jesus. Jesus comes to restore our humanity through His, but we are not Jesus. We can be entirely well-intentioned, but if we attempt to pursue even humility apart from Him, we will simply act out of our own pride once again. The temptation is so real and so prevalent that Paul continues:

> Therefore [because of Jesus' humble obedience] God has highly exalted him and bestowed on him the name that is above every name, so that at the name of Jesus every knee should bow, in heaven and on earth and under the earth, and every tongue confess that Jesus Christ is Lord, to the glory of God the Father.[26]

And suddenly we see where we fit in the narrative: facedown in the dust.

We are not called to embody Jesus ourselves; He has already been incarnated and is still even now! No, we are not called to be Jesus; we are called to fall at His feet and worship Him. We are called to affirm that "the Word became flesh and dwelt among us, and we have seen his glory, glory as of the only Son from the Father, full of grace and truth."[27] And it is through this worship, through recognizing *His* rightful place, that we are finally humbled.

When we are consumed with God's glory, we forget to worry about our own. When our eyes are fixed on Him as the source of all goodness and truth and beauty, we accept that we are not. When we are enamored by His worth and majesty, we can stop being so enamored with ourselves. And fascinatingly, when we seek God's glory, we'll be able to appreciate it in the people around us. Instead of seeing them as threats to our own glory, we will see them as beautiful reflections of His.

---

26. Philippians 2:9–11.
27. John 1:14.

And suddenly the world is wide enough. Suddenly "this world surely is wide enough to hold both thee and me."[28] Instead of competing, we can care for each other. Instead of comparing ourselves, we can have compassion on each other. Instead of controlling each other, we can cultivate each other.

Tree of Life

"No tree can grow except on the root from which it sprang . . .
If humility is the root of the tree, its nature must be seen
in every branch, leaf, and fruit." —Andrew Murray

In her book *None Like Him*, Bible teacher Jen Wilkin writes that

> we must recover the truth that was obscured by the serpent: rather than being like God in His unlimited Divinity, we are to be like God in our limited humanity. . . . We are limited by design, in order that our limits might point us to worship our limitless God. . . . When I reach the limit of my strength, I worship the One whose strength never flags. When I reach the limit of my reason, I worship the One whose reason is beyond searching out.[29]

The rest of *Humble Roots* is dedicated to exploring how living within these limits brings rest. We'll see how humility informs our understanding of ourselves and each other—how it changes how we think about our bodies, our minds, even our ambition. The goal is—as Lewis put it—to get "rid of all the silly nonsense

---

28. From Laurence Sterne's *The Life and Opinions of Tristram Shandy, Gentleman*, Book II, Ch. 12 (1760).
29. Jen Wilkin, *None Like Him: 10 Ways God Is Different from Us* (and *Why That's a Good Thing*) (Wheaton, IL: Crossway, 2016), 11.

about your own dignity which has made you restless and unhappy all your life."[30]

But this is no quick fix. What we're after is sustainable growth. The kind of growth that happens over a lifetime of encountering and learning from Jesus' own humility. We're on a search to recover humility and enjoy its fruit once again.

---

30. C. S. Lewis, *Mere Christianity: Comprising The Case for Christianity, Christian Behaviour, and Beyond Personality* (New York: Touchstone, 1996), 114.

II

For thus says the LORD, "Behold,
I will extend peace to her like a river,
and the glory of the nations like an overflowing
stream. . . . You shall see, and your heart shall
rejoice; your bones shall flourish like the grass."

—ISAIAH 66:12,14

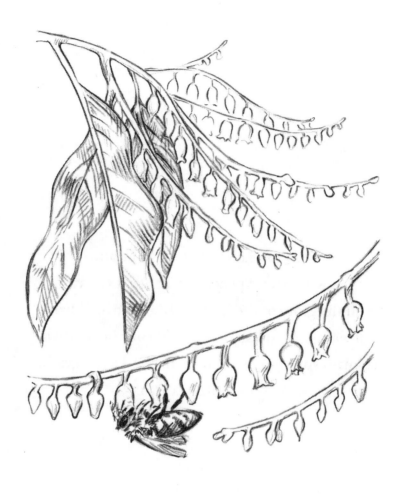

FIGURE 5

Sourwood tree, *Oxydendrum arboretum*

Chapter 5

Local Honey

*"I shouldn't think even millionaires could eat anything
nicer than new bread and real butter and honey for tea."*
—Dodie Smith

"DO Y' LIKE HONEY?"
As his voice boomed through the sanctuary which was, by
this time, nearly full, I realized that Russ had forgotten his hearing
aid again. It was just moments before eleven o'clock, and as usual
I was scurrying down the center aisle to my seat—second pew
back from the front on the organ side—when Russ stopped me.
The musicians had already started the prelude, but I paused and
turned toward him. He had always been a large man, but lately,
he'd become stooped, his chest appearing more caved in every
time I saw him. His skin was spotted with age, and he wore a ban-
dage where doctors had recently removed a spot of skin cancer.

"YES, RUSS," I bellowed back, carefully articulating each
word. "WE LOVE HONEY."

He smiled, his eyes crinkled, and he nodded his head in ac-
knowledgment and affirmation.

"GOOD! I GOT SOME FER Y' AN' TH' PREACHER." He
thrust a glass quart jar into my hands. "IT'S FROM MY BAR-

BER AN' IT'S TH' BEST HONEY Y' EVER TASTED!"

With that Russ slipped back to his own pew and I hurried to mine, both of us just settling in as the last notes of the prelude died away. Such culinary gifts were not unusual from Russ. When we'd first met, he was in his mid-eighties, widowed, and retired from the railroad. "It wasn't a career," he'd tell us on the days he remembered his hearing aid and could converse normally. "It was a love affair." In his retirement, Russ tinkered with model trains, came to church, and baked. Many Sundays we'd find a brown paper bag on our pew; it might hold biscuits or rolls or a pie. And on very special occasions, Russ would slip me a box of chocolates with a wink and a promise not to tell my husband.

But this Sunday, it was local honey. Sweet nectar of the gods.

For most of human history, all honey was local—a product of the blossoming plants within the immediate area of the humans who consumed it. Because of this, local honeys vary widely in color and flavor based on the plants within the bees' gathering range. These plants include the wildflowers that most of us imagine (like clover), but they also include many other nectar-producing plants from garden vegetables and field crops to flowering trees like sourwood, chestnut, tulip poplar, locust, and maple. Much like wines that are a product of the growing conditions of a specific region, local honey captures the unique ecological composition of an area, leading some to claim it can even ward off seasonal allergies.

Because of their distinctive flavors and health benefits, local honeys have become something of a gastronomic trend, but interest in local honey is also tied to the broader farm-to-table movement, a movement that prioritizes food that is sustainable, organic, local, and ethical. You might know this movement in terms of clean food, whole food, slow food, or real food; some call it living close to the land. And while few of us actually live on homesteads, the interest in food sourcing is sending many a suburban homemaker in search of bootleg raw milk, educating herself on the difference between grass-fed and grain-fed beef, and shopping for local honey at weekend farmers' markets.

Ironically, most folks in my community wouldn't consider themselves part of the farm-to-table movement, local honey notwithstanding. They're locavores to an extent, but they're not particularly worried about refined flour or antibiotics, unless they need them to fight the bronchitis that's working its way to pneumonia. And even if they wanted to buy organic, they simply couldn't afford to. In many ways, the jar that Russ handed me that Sunday tells our story. The label reads simply:

PURE HONEY

from the bees of Wade Sutphin

That's it. No celebratory announcements about being locally sourced or organic or sustainable. No claims to health benefits or fair trade or doing good. In many ways, beekeepers like Wade Sutphin aren't trying to recover a way of life because they never lost it. Around here, you live close to the land because the land is what you've been given, and you take care of what you've been given. You raise your own vegetables because your granddaddy did, and seeds are cheaper than produce shipped from Mexico. You hunt because you like venison, and the deer have been eating your hostas again.

And you buy local honey because your barber sells it, and it's the best honey you ever tasted.

Body of Earth

*"If a man is rich and strong anywhere, it must
be on his native soil." —Henry David Thoreau*

In many ways, this no-nonsense approach to the land hearkens
back to Genesis 1:28. After forming mankind in His image, God
commissions the man and woman to "Be fruitful and multiply and
fill the earth and subdue it, and have dominion over the fish of the
sea and over the birds of the heavens and over every living thing
that moves on the earth." As image bearers, human beings are to
rule and reign in God's stead, taking personal responsibility for the
earth. But this creation mandate is not a call to ownership; it is a
call to *stewardship*. To the humble recognition that you "take care
of what you've been given," regardless of whether it is a quarter
acre in a subdivision or 150 acres of family land.

Or even the real estate of your own body.

You may have never thought of stewarding your body as part
of the call to steward the earth, but it's not that much of a stretch.
We are, after all, made from the earth, a mixture of minerals and
elements that have only been made alive by the quickening Spirit
of God. As well, the success of our bodies (our ability to be fruitful and multiply) is intrinsically connected with the success of
the earth. "It is hardly surprising then," writes naturalist Wendell
Berry, "that there should be some profound resemblances between
our treatment of our bodies and the treatment of the earth."[1] So
how do we "take care of what we've been given"? How does humility inform how we steward our bodies?

The first thing humility teaches you is to honor the physicality
of your body. That your body is physical may seem self-evident.

---

1. Wendell Berry, "The Body and the Earth," in *The Art of the Commonplace: Agrarian
Essays of Wendell Berry*, ed. Norman Wirzba (Washington, DC: Counterpoint, 2003), 93.

When we use the word "body," we're talking about the material part of you that is distinct from (although intrinsically connected to) the immaterial part. The issue, of course, is not whether we recognize our bodies as physical, but whether we recognize this physical nature as good. Do we humbly embrace and honor our bodies, or do we see them as a source of shame, embarrassment, and guilt? "Many people," notes biblical scholar Dr. Gregg Allison, "abhor their body, and many Christians . . . consider their body to be, at best, a hindrance to spiritual maturity and, at worst, inherently evil or the ultimate source of sin."[2]

In fact, noted researcher Brené Brown identifies body image ("how we think and feel about our bodies") as an almost universal source of shame. And while the root of this shame is as diverse as our own experiences and insecurities, it is exacerbated by the messages we receive from broader culture and sometimes even from the church.[3] Flip open a fashion magazine or scroll through your social media feed, and you'll be bombarded with image after image of perfectly sculpted, flawless bodies and the inherent judgment that comes with them. As a result, soon-to-be brides obsess over pre-wedding diets, new mothers stress over "getting my body back" within weeks of giving birth, and entire industries are dedicated to preventing the natural process of aging.

Within the church, the messages can be just as mixed. Women are simultaneously celebrated for being "smoking hot wives" at the same time they are told that their bodies are a source of temptation, a ticking time bomb that, for love of their brothers, they

2. Gregg Allison, "Toward a Theology of Human Embodiment," *Southern Baptist Journal of Theology*, 13/2 (Summer 2009), http://www.sbts.edu/wp-content/uploads/sites/5/2009/10/sbjt-2009summer-allison.pdf.
3. To be clear, I am discussing the general sense of shame that corresponds to body image—the shame we experience from the limitations, imperfections, and changes of our bodies. I am not addressing the shame that accompanies physical and sexual trauma in which a person must find wholeness after a profound and ungodly violation of his or her body.

must defuse. Men experience shame over their bodies, as well; they may believe themselves too short, too thin, too heavy, to have too much body hair, to have not enough facial hair, or to lack muscle tone. Men also receive confusing messages about sexuality: On the one hand, a natural appreciation for beauty becomes equated with lust, resulting in shame for even noticing the attractiveness of a woman (or another man). But when age causes a man's sex drive to wane, the same shame tells him to seek out small blue pills to recover his manhood.

The result is a widespread and profound rejection of the goodness of our physical bodies. "In fact," Brown concludes in an essay titled "Shame and Body Image,"

> body shame is so powerful and often so deeply rooted . . . that it impacts why and how we feel shame in many of the other categories. . . . When "our very own bodies" fill us with disgust and feelings of worthlessness, shame can fundamentally change who we are and how we approach the world.[4]

And so we neglect our bodies because we don't believe they are worth stewarding. We are uncomfortable in our own skin because we believe it a constant source of temptation. And we chase emotional and spiritual experiences that allow us to escape, if only for a few moments, these prisons of earth.

But are we meant to escape our bodies—are we meant to escape the very thing that God designed and called "good"?

---

4. Brené Brown, "Shame and Body Image" at Mothers Movement Online, November 2004, http://www.mothersmovement.org/features/body_image/b_brown_body_shame.htm.

Unashamed

"And God saw everything that he had made,
and behold, it was very good." —Genesis 1:31

The first scriptural reference to body shame occurs immediately after the man and woman consume the forbidden fruit. Prior to this, God has blessed the bodies of the man and woman and they exist "naked and not ashamed." But after they consume the forbidden fruit, "the eyes of both were opened, and they knew that they were naked"[5] and tried to cover themselves. The natural question is "Why?" Why the sudden shame over their bodies? What had changed?

The most significant thing that changed was that the man and woman had lifted themselves up in pride, desiring to be like God. But instead of making them like God, the fruit revealed how *un-*like God they were. Suddenly they could see clearly, and their bodies were a glaring, painful reminder of their creaturehood and their attempted rebellion. If pride told them that they could be like God, their physical bodies told them in no uncertain terms that they absolutely could not.

And so after my Sunday school class at Small Brick Church learns about the creation and the fall, and after we've colored the apples red, we also learn this catechism:

"Does God have a body?"

"No, God is a spirit and does not have a body like man."

We learn our limits. We learn that we are not like God. We learn humility.

Rejecting our physical bodies, flawed as they are, is rooted in the same pride that desires to "ascend to heaven" and be like God,

---

5. Genesis 3:7.

the same pride that desires to live beyond natural human limits. So while culture sells us the lie that our bodies could be flawless, we buy it because of our pride. We buy the lie that we could be eternal, always ageless, never wrinkling, never growing old. We buy the lie that we could be omnipotent, always virile, never tiring, never needing rest. We buy the lie that we could be omnipresent, always available, never distant, never missing out. And when our bodies remind us that we are not, when they wrinkle and sag and weaken, we are ashamed of them.

We do not hate our bodies for what they are; we hate them for what they are not. We hate them for not being godlike. We hate them for being imperfect. We hate them for being limited. And like the man and woman in the garden, instead of rejecting the pride that tells us we could be like God, we reject our bodies that tell us we cannot.

This is why the incarnation is so significant; this is why it was necessary for Jesus to be "born in the likeness of men and [be] found in human form."[6] To reclaim humility, Jesus embraced human limits as good. To restore our humanity, Jesus revealed the goodness of being bound in space and time. To free us from shame, Jesus proved that being human is nothing to be ashamed of. "Who, though he was in the form of God, did not count equality with God a thing to be grasped. . ."[7] And to show us the goodness of being made a creature, Jesus showed us that equality with God is not a fruit we should even be tempted to reach up and pluck.

In her essay, Brown notes that the first step to reconciling our physical shame is "to acknowledge our secret goals and expectations." Theologically speaking, this means acknowledging our secret goal and expectation of perfection. Many of us are grasping

---

6. Philippians 2:6–8.
7. Ibid.

for a transcendence that is humanly impossible. Humility reminds us of our limits; humility teaches us that we are physical beings existing in a broken world. Not only are we limited and imperfect ourselves, but our bodies and our sense of our bodies have been shaped by the false messages around us. Simply learning to "love your body" will not free you from shame because, at times, your body will feel very unlovable. What will free you from shame is humility; what will free you from shame is accepting that you are not and were never meant to be divine.

And once you do, you are free to embrace your physical nature. You are free to stop obsessing over your imperfections because you know that to be human is to be imperfect. You are free to enjoy your unique genetic makeup that has been generations in the making. You are free to reject the lies that have made you ashamed—whether they come from the media, friends and family, or your own head. You are free to hear the voice of the only one whose opinion counts.

You are free to hear God declare your body "good."

Pure Honey

*"He shall eat curds and honey when he knows how
to refuse the evil and choose the good."* ——*Isaiah 7:15*

Besides emphasizing local stewardship, the farm-to-table movement also promotes the ethical production and consumption of food. This covers a variety of practices, but in its most basic sense, an ethical food network harms neither the earth, the producers, nor the consumers. Within the honey industry, ethical practices include accurately sourcing and labeling honey. If a quart jar of honey, like the one that Russ gave me, says that it's "P U R E   H O N E Y," then it had better be pure, unadulterated honey. For large scale distributors, this means tracing their supply back to its origins; but as more and more honey is imported from places as far away as India and China, this is increasingly difficult. Without strict oversight, what is labeled "pure honey" may in fact be a blend of honey and cane sugar or a honey-flavored syrup.

To be fair, the temptation to adulterate honey is not unique to the global marketplace. Wherever human beings exist, there will also exist the temptation to one-up each other. In a 1983 oral history of Mr. Adam Clement, a traditional beekeeper from Ararat, Virginia, the interviewer asks Mr. Clement about those who sell honey that is less than pure. Clement, who'd been keeping bees in the Blue Ridge since the Depression, confirmed that he knew folks who'd make a "sugar water with alum, which creates a syrup. This way, a little bit of honey will go a long way but the result is no more than honey flavored sugar water that looks like clear honey."[8] Clement quickly adds that he, himself, "sells it like [he] gets it."

For beekeepers like Clement, ethics is not a complicated business; it does not require certifications or oversight boards. You simply "sell it like you get it," and being a gentleman of honor is enough to ensure that his honey will always be pure. Later, when the interviewer wondered how Clement could label honey a certain variety—like "sourwood honey"—without knowing which flowers every bee visited, Clement offered a simple explanation: "If you take a sourwood blossom and switch the back of your hand with it, small drops of nectar will appear on your hand. This is what sourwood honey will taste like and if it doesn't, then it's not sourwood."

Mr. Clement's highly developed palate and his being a man

---

8. Bob Heafner, "Adam Clement—Beekeeper," *The Mountain Laurel*, September 1983, http://www.mtnlaurel.com/arts-and-crafts/118-mr-adam-clement-beekeeper.html.

of his word hearkens back to simpler times when community in-frastructure ensured purity. If a beekeeper tried to sell something other than "pure honey," everyone would know. But today, when most of us are distanced from our food sources, regulation and truth in labeling laws are a necessity. In absence of a platoon of Mr. Clements, some states are enacting stricter labeling guidelines, in-cluding the provision that honey labeled "sourwood honey" must contain at least 51 percent sourwood nectar (*Oxydendrum arbore-tum*) to be confirmed by laboratory testing.[9]

In many ways, the ethics of honey tells the larger story of hu-man competition and our attempts to regulate human behavior. When God made mankind in His image, He made us dependent on each other. Just as food producers and consumers are depen-dent on each other, our mutual success is bound up in each other. And one of the most obvious examples of this mutual dependence is found in our physical bodies, in our biological maleness and femaleness. Our bodies themselves teach us that we are meant to work cooperatively for the good of each other and the broader community. In fact, the very differences between us are given to enable us to steward the earth, "to be fruitful and multiply" in both a literal and an archetypal sense. It's not surprising then, that when pride enters the picture, the very thing designed to unite us turns into a source of division and competition.

The first hint of the competition between men and women occurs immediately after the fall. Instead of finding their male-ness and femaleness a source of flourishing and blessing, the man and woman now find their differences a source of temptation. In Genesis 3:16 God warns the woman: "Your desire shall be for

---

9. Part of the reason beekeepers might be tempted to fudge on labeling is that sourwood honey is somewhat rare and highly desirable. In fact, in 2005 and 2007, the distinct taste of native Appalachian sourwood honey won the designation "Best Honey in the World" from Apimonda, the International Federation of Beekeepers' Associations.

your husband, and he shall rule over you." Theologians offer many different interpretations of this text (some more convoluted than others), but you don't have to be a theologian to understand the real-world implications. You must simply look at how men and women use their biological differences—how we use our bodies— to compete.

Generally speaking, men are physically stronger than women and so their natural temptation would be to use their strength to control women. We see this every time a man physically abuses or assaults a woman. We see it every time a man uses his power to harass or intimidate a woman. But we also see it every time a man walks away from a woman who is pregnant with his child. When he abandons her, he is taking advantage of the fact that an infant grows inside its mother and not its father. In a broken world where might makes right, the physical makeup of a man's body gives him an advantage that a woman will never have.[10]

To compensate, women may be tempted to capitalize on the one thing they have that men want. A woman may not be as phys- ically powerful as a man, but she alone has the capacity to bear life. Her fertility (and by extension her sexuality) is a potential source of power. Because men desire her, she will be tempted to objectify herself to capture their attention. Instead of deriving her worth, value, and authority from being made in God's image, she will be tempted to derive it from men. When a woman flaunts her sexuality, she does not necessarily want to be reduced to a sex ob-

---

10. The biological differences between men and women are part of the reason abortion exists. Through the act of abortion, women mimic the same biological "freedom" that men possess naturally. After a child is conceived, a man may or may not choose to stay with the mother, but nothing physically binds him to her. And so, instead of shouldering the responsibility, many walk away. Unfortunately, instead of correcting this, abortion enables women to practice the same type of abandonment, which in turn continues and exacer- bates the cycle of not holding men responsible to care for the children they create. If there is simply no child, he's off the hook entirely.

ject, but she's learned, if only by instinct, that this is how a woman can rule in a broken world.

These gender dynamics play out in larger, systematic ways as we collectively celebrate unrestrained masculine power and encourage overt displays of female sexuality. We cheer for men who can beat other men to a pulp, and we applaud women who use their bodies to compete with each other. And the very things that were given to unite us—our biological differences—now divide us. The problem is so real and so dangerous that Christians often feel the need to establish standards of deportment for men and women. We tell women they must dress a certain way and make exacting pronouncements about what is modest and what is not. We tell men they must not have female friends, confirming for them that all women are attempting to control them through their sexuality. We tell both to be suspicious of the other, always looking for the deeper motive behind a gesture, a look, or an outfit.

But in so doing, we miss the larger point: Beekeeper Adam Clement doesn't sell "pure honey" because a state passed a regulation; Mr. Clement sells "pure honey" because he is a man of honor.

The problem, of course, is that while external laws can establish a standard of quality or behavior, they have no power to actually make beekeepers do the right thing. Government may try to enforce such standards (although this itself will prove challenging), but the standards themselves cannot produce the internal ethics that motivate Adam Clement to "sell it like he gets it." So too, we can construct regulations about what we should or shouldn't put in our bodies or what we should or shouldn't put on our bodies or where we should or shouldn't go with our bodies; but these regulations won't make us ethical people. These regulations can't heal the divide between men and women. These regulations cannot bring peace to the gender wars.

In his letter to the church at Colossae, the apostle Paul addresses the ineffectiveness of such rules to change human behavior. A particular faction had gained power by promoting a type of asceticism that they claimed would curb the lust of the flesh. When other believers didn't follow their particular rules, they passed judgment on them and disqualified them as "true" believers. But Paul fires back that such regulations don't actually have the power to transform us. Such "human precepts and teachings," he writes, "have indeed an appearance of wisdom in promoting self-made religion and asceticism and severity to the body, but they are of no value in stopping the indulgence of the flesh."[11]

Underneath the Colossians' legalism was a profound and certain trust in themselves. They believed they could reach purity by adhering to certain standards of behavior. Paul writes that instead of "holding fast to the Head [Christ], from whom the whole body . . . grows with a growth that is from God," they were holding fast to their regulations, entirely confident of their ability to reach them. In other words, they were proud. "The chief mark of counterfeit holiness," writes Andrew Murray, "is its lack of humility. . . . The great test of whether the holiness we profess to seek or to attain is truth and life will be *whether it produces an increasing humility in us*."[12]

Ultimately the Colossians' pride was revealed by what they were looking at, by what had captured their attention. Instead of being concerned with eternal realities, they were concerned with regulating temporary realities. Instead of being consumed with Christ's glory, they were consumed with their own. But it is only by beholding Christ that we are changed. It is only by beholding Christ who Himself took "*on the form of a servant*" that we learn to serve each other. We do not break the cycle of manipulation and control by trying to regulate male/female relationships. We break the cycle by

---

11. Colossians 2:23.
12. Andrew Murray's book *Humility* was first published in 1895.

turning both men and women's eyes to Christ. "If then you have been raised with Christ," Paul continues, "seek the things that are above, where Christ is. . . . Set your minds on things that are above, not on things that are on the earth." And when we do, when we see "Christ who is our life," we are humbled. And it is this humility, not pride, that changes us. It is this humility, not pride, that makes us ethical people. And it is this humility that enables us to answer the call in the very next verse to put to death "sexual immorality, impurity, passion, evil desire, and covetousness."[13]

Because it is humility, not pride, that leads to purity.

Once we are humble people, we won't need external regulations to force us to sell "pure honey." We will be people of honor who are safe with one another; we will put away "anger, wrath, malice, slander, and obscene talk."[14] Once we are humble people, we will no longer use our bodies to compete with each other because we will have put on a "new self, which is being renewed in knowledge after the image of its creator."[15] Once we are humble people, men will no longer feel the need to prove their dominance and women will no longer feel desperate to be physically desirable. We will use our bodies to serve each other. And our love for one another will be pure.

Raised Imperishable

"It is not the soul . . . that will rise but the body, glorified."
—*Flannery O'Connor*

"Y' KNOW THEY FOUND HONEY IN THE PHARAOH'S TOMB?" Russ bellowed at me one Sunday upon handing me

---

13. The entirety of Paul's argument against the legalists at Colossae, and how true purity is attained, is found in Colossians 2:8–3:17.
14. Colossians 3:8.
15. Colossians 3:10.

another jar of Wade Sutphin's liquid gold. I answered that no, I had not, which was a natural invitation for him to continue. "IT'D BEN THERE THOUSAN' O' YEARS AN' NEVER SPOILT! IT'S 'CAUSE HONEY CAN'T GO BAD." He pointed a bony finger at the jar in my hands and nodded his head. "Y' KEEP'AT ON T' SHELF AN' IT'LL BE GOOD FER YEARS."

Russ passed away this last winter one day after his ninetieth birthday. Before he died, he suffered through an extended period of illness, lost a tremendous amount of weight, and was hardly recognizable. The strapping man who fought in World War II, raised a family, worked on the railroad, and brought me local honey seemed to evaporate before our very eyes. The life literally sucked out of him. *"If [God] should set his heart to it and gather to himself his spirit and his breath, all flesh would perish together, and man would return to dust."*[16]

At the funeral, I couldn't bring myself to walk to his casket. My vantage point from the pew was enough. Because even as we mourned, even as we sang "Blessed Assurance," and folks talked about the "real" Russ not being there, I knew better. I knew this separation of body and soul wasn't right. Part of Russ was some-where else, but part of him was still with us. In his body, he had lived and loved and died and to tell ourselves otherwise was cold comfort.

If these bodies don't matter, what does? No, these bodies, as flawed and limited as they are, do matter, and that is why we grieve so much when we see our loved ones separated from themselves. It is also why we cling to the hope that one day body and soul will be reunited. It is why we cling to the hope of the resurrection. It is why we cling to these words: "For the trumpet will sound, and

---

16. Job 34:14–15.

the dead will be raised imperishable, and we shall be changed. For this perishable body must put on the imperishable, and this mortal body must put on immortality."[17] As imperishable as sweet, local honey.

And so it is why, with generations of saints who have laid their own loved ones in the earth, both far and near; who themselves lie there awaiting the resurrection, we affirm: "I believe in the resurrection of the *body*, and life everlasting. Amen."[18]

And amen.

---

17. 1 Corinthians 15:52–53.
18. From the Apostles' Creed.

FIGURE 6

Sweet Basil, *Ocimum basilicum*

Chapter 6

Healing Herbs

"Wherever possible, choose sunny, even land that slopes gently to the south or east. For convenience, a kitchen garden should be close to the house." —The Shaker Book of the Garden, 1843

One Mother's Day, I convinced my husband to help me start an herb garden. We'd been growing herbs halfheartedly for several years—a few pots of mint on the patio, small clumps of cilantro near the tomatoes—but I decided that I wanted a proper kitchen garden. I wanted a space just outside my door where I could mix flowers, herbs, and smaller vegetables. The French would know such a space as *un jardin potager*, the Scots as a *kailyard*; but for me, a kitchen garden was a matter of convenience and necessity. A kitchen garden is so named, not simply because of what grows in it, but because of its proximity to the cooking workspace. In my case, a kitchen garden should be close enough to the back door so that when I remember mid-recipe that I've forgotten basil, I can slip outside, snip a few stems, and be back in time to stir the sauce before it burns.

So one weekend in the middle of May, Nathan and I stopped by a local greenhouse to get started. Wandering through the metal growing benches, my mind was a whirl of possibilities: mint for tea and jelly, cilantro for fresh salsa and guacamole, basil for pesto, caprese salad, and lemonade, and rosemary and thyme for roast chicken. By the time we finished, my kitchen garden would also include lavender, lemongrass, dill, both curled and flat parsley, and pineapple sage (which surprisingly tastes very much like pineapple).

In modern parlance, herbs are distinguished from other edible plants by the intensity of their flavor and aroma, a quality that also makes them naturally pest-resistant. The comparatively high concentration of essential or volatile oils in herbs is why we will fill a salad with lettuce, spinach, and arugula, but we'd never consider eating the same quantity of mint, sage, and basil. The concentration of oils is also why herbs have been used in perfumes, as seasoning, and in medicine throughout human history. Their flavor is so alluring, in fact, that whenever I pass my herb garden, I find it nearly impossible to resist breaking off a sprig of lavender, rubbing it between my palms, and inhaling deeply. And when on the regular occasion I find a stalk of my *Ocimum basilicum* stripped of its leaves, I know my nine-year-old son has succumbed to the same temptation and is somewhere happily chewing on a plug of basil.

The versatility of herbs has earned them the moniker "friend of physicians and praise of cooks,"[1] and throughout history, human beings have used them to promote both physical and emotional well-being. Knowledge of beneficial plants was often passed down orally from generation to generation, but physicians from the Roman Empire to the Middle East to Moorish Africa long cataloged their therapeutic benefits, and written records from the Far East date back to 3000 BC. During the Middle Ages, herbs

---

1. This phrase has been attributed to both Charlemagne and his tutor, Alcuin.

became the purview of religious orders when nuns and monks cultivated "physick" gardens as part of cloistered life.

With the emergence of modern science in the seventeenth century, however, traditional herbalism came under scrutiny because it was so often mixed with folk superstition and astrology. (Word on the street during the Middle Ages was that wearing buttercups in a bag around your neck would cure insanity.) As science developed, the study of herbs and their uses fell into the separate (although overlapping) fields of botany and modern pharmacology. Today, these fields are merging once again in the growing interest in essential oils and aromatherapy. Thousands of years after those first Chinese physicians recorded their observations about the physical and emotional benefits of herbs, many a middle-class, Western housewife could tell you to use mint to stimulate your senses, lavender to relieve anxiety, and lemon balm to cure insomnia. And if you're struggling with mental clarity, take Ophelia's advice from Hamlet: "There's rosemary, that's for remembrance."

Whatever the link between these piquant plants and our inner life,[2] it presents interesting questions about the nature of emotions and spiritual formation. Specific to this conversation, what effect does cultivating humility have on a healthy emotional life? Are feelings simply a matter of biochemistry, or can humility offer a guide through the shadows and vagaries of emotion?

---

2. Clinical research is still limited, but the University of Maryland Medical Center notes that "some experts believe our sense of smell may play a role [in aromatherapy]. The 'smell' receptors in your nose communicate with parts of your brain (the amygdala and hippocampus) that serve as storehouses for emotions and memories. When you breathe in essential oil molecules, some researchers believe they stimulate these parts of your brain and influence physical, emotional, and mental health." http://umm.edu/health/medical/altmed/treatment/aromatherapy.

Authentic Selves

One of the challenges to understanding how humility shapes our emotional life is simply understanding what emotions are. Throughout history, what we now term "emotions" have been referred to as humors, passions, appetites, affections, and sentiments. Thomas Dixon, director of the Queen Mary Centre for the History of the Emotions in London, notes that the word "emotion" didn't even enter the English lexicon until the eighteenth century and at the time simply referred to a "physical disturbance." It was only in the late 1800s with the emergence of clinical psychology that the term "emotions" began to refer to our inner or mental life.[3]

Still, while linguists and researchers may struggle to define what emotions are, we know them when we see (or feel) them. We know fear, disgust, anger, surprise, happiness, sadness, embarrassment, excitement, contempt, shame, satisfaction, confidence, and amusement. We know the breadth and depth of them, the variety of their flavors and intensity. Some sharp, some sweet, some bitter. We also understand how emotions drive our decisions. We understand how shame can cause a person to hide away, how anger can lead to destructive behavior, or how fear can trap us in abusive relationships. Emotions are so powerful, in fact, that Stoics in the ancient world suggested that we deny them altogether and only make decisions out of reason. With the rise of Christian philosophy, however, men like Augustine and eventually Thomas Aquinas offered an alternative reading of emotions—through Christ, our evil passions can be transformed to holy affections. Through Christ, apathy can become compassion and lust can become love.

And this transformation begins with humility.

Remember that humility, itself, is not an emotional state.

---

3. Thomas Dixon, "'Emotion': The History of a Keyword in Crisis," *Emotion Review* 4 (2012): 338–44.

Humility is not feeling a certain way about yourself, not *feeling* small or low or embarrassed or even humiliated. Theologically speaking, humility is a proper understanding of who God is and who we are as a result. We may feel certain things because of this understanding—we may feel safe in the care of our Creator or we may feel fear when we disobey Him—but these emotions are the result of our reverence for God. As American theologian and Puritan pastor Jonathan Edwards writes,

> Holy affections are not heat without light; but evermore arise from the information of the understanding, some spiritual instruction that the mind receives, some light or actual knowledge. The child of God is graciously affected, because he sees and understands something more of divine things than he did before, more of God or Christ, and of the glorious things exhibited in the gospel.[4]

In other words, we do not resolve our emotional uncertainty—our stress and anxiety—by focusing on our emotions themselves. We resolve our uncertainty by getting to the root cause. We resolve it by learning from Jesus, who is meek and lowly of heart.

The premise of this book is that much of our emotional instability is rooted in pride. Not simply pride in our intellect or our physical bodies, but a pride that prioritizes our emotions as the source of truth. To understand this, we need look no further than to our cultural fixation with emotional authenticity. Authenticity, as we've come to understand it, celebrates "telling it like it is" and encourages you to "be true to yourself." But today, being true to yourself doesn't mean making an honest evaluation of yourself; it means embracing your emotional experience of the world as truth. As one young adult put it, "Morality is how I feel too,

---

4. Jonathan Edwards, *The Religious Affections* (1746; repr. Mineola: Dover Publications, 2013), 192.

because in my heart, I could feel it. Most of the time . . . I feel it in my heart, and it makes it easier for me to morally decide what's right and wrong. . . . And if it feels good, then I'm going to do it."[5]

Authentic truth, then, is found "within ourselves or must at least resonate with our one-of-a-kind personality,"[6] writes Jonathan Grant in his book *Divine Sex*. Tracing our fixation with authenticity through romantic relationships, Grant shows how we can become trapped in our own emotional experiences. For example, when you struggle to feel proper love toward your spouse, it is not enough to fight to maintain the marriage. "Truth," as defined by our emotions, demands that you express your lack of romantic connection and even leave the marriage. "Worse still," Grant writes, authenticity teaches us "if we stay together in the face of romantic eclipse, then our children, if we have them, will be polluted by our hypocrisy. It is really in their best interests that we move on to new things."[7]

But what if prioritizing our emotional experience is what leads to our emotional chaos in the first place? What if, given the lack of external reality, we have become enslaved to our emotions?

And here is how humility brings rest to our internal life: Humility teaches us that "God is greater than our heart."[8] Humility teaches us that we don't have to obey our emotions because the only version of reality that matters is God's.

To understand how we can get trapped by our emotions, consider what happens when you learn a friend has been talking about you behind your back. You probably feel anger, pain, and

---

5. Christian Smith and Patricia Snell, *Souls in Transition: The Religious and Spiritual Lives of Emerging Adults* (Oxford: Oxford University Press, 2009), 51.

6. Jonathan Grant, *Divine Sex: A Compelling Vision for Christian Relationships in a Hypersexualized Age* (Grand Rapids: Brazos Press, 2015), 30.

7. Ibid., 31.

8. 1 John 3:20.

fear. At least, I would. I'd be angered by the duplicity and want to strike back. I'd be hurt by what they think of me and cling to others for reassurance. And because I'd fear that other people might believe my friend's claims, I'd rush around trying to correct their impression of me. And I would do all this, not because it is the wisest course of action, but because my emotions are driving me to protect myself. But what if humility roots our sense of self in something—or Someone—greater than our emotions? What if humility could free us from obsessing about how other people feel about us or even how we feel about ourselves?

In 1 Corinthians 4, Paul shows how humility moves our sense of self away from our emotions and places it were it belongs:

> But with me it is a very small thing that I should be judged by you or by any human court. In fact, I do not even judge myself. For I am not aware of anything against myself, but I am not thereby acquitted. It is the Lord who judges me.[9]

In other words, your judgment of me doesn't matter. My judgment of myself doesn't matter either. The only person whose judgment counts is the Lord's. He's the only one who can accurately understand my heart (even I can't understand it), and I trust Him to judge and reward faithfully. Commenting on this passage, Tim Keller writes that the humble "person would never be hurt particularly badly by criticism. It would not devastate them, it would not keep them up late. . . . A person who is devastated by criticism is putting too much value on what other people think, on other people's opinions."[10]

---

9. 1 Corinthians 4:3–4.
10. Timothy Keller, *The Freedom of Self-Forgetfulness: The Path to True Christian Joy* (Chorley, England: 10Publishing, 2012), 33.

"God is greater than our heart."

And suddenly you see how humility frees us. Because God's judgment is paramount, I do not have to worry about my friend's judgment of me. Instead of responding out of anger, I can rest in God's judgment of me through Christ. Instead of responding to the pain of being misunderstood, I can rest in the fact that God understands me even better than I understand myself. And instead of rushing around to convince everyone of my upstanding character, I can rest in God's ability to vindicate (or correct) me. And suddenly I am freed from anger, pain, and fear. Suddenly I am free to respond to difficult circumstances from a place of control and grace. Suddenly I'm free to see the world from a perspective larger than my own heart.

Holy Audacity

"Many a times I find my patients disturbed by trouble of Conscience or Sorrow, and I have to act the Divine before I can be the Physician. In fact our greatest skill lies in the infusion of Hopes, to induce confidence and peace of mind." —Nicholas Culpeper, seventeenth-century herbalist and English Puritan

Within twenty-four hours of putting in my herb garden, more than half the plants had died. I was devastated. And embarrassed. When I first broached the idea of an herb garden with Nathan, I promised him that I'd take responsibility for it. This would be my "bit of earth" and to prove my commitment, I did the majority of the work myself, even preparing and digging the ground by hand. I knew Nathan had his doubts—after all, I sometimes struggle to keep houseplants alive—but this was my chance to prove myself. So I went to the library to research herbs and brought home stacks of books. I made a list of the varieties I wanted, and the

Saturday after we'd bought them, I gave the soil one final turn and transplanted and watered them. I even mulched the bed for good measure.

But the next morning, I was met with a horticultural train wreck. Plants that only a day before were alive and flourishing were now sickly and limp. The leaves I'd hoped to turn into culinary and apothecary glory were scorched and dropping from the stems. And the only thing that had changed was that I had touched them. I felt terrible. Not only was my pride hurt, but we'd spent nearly seventy-five dollars and I'd put in hours of work. All for nothing. I'd failed. It was all my fault.

Except that it wasn't.

After an hour of frantic searching online, I stumbled on a description of my poor burnt herbs: "Damage resembles that caused by drought, poor drainage, fertilizer burn, or pesticide misapplication. Symptoms include yellowing of leaf edges, scorched-looking leaves, defoliation, and/or death of plants."[11] It turns out I'd spread "sour" mulch on my garden.

Apparently, mulch sours when it decomposes without enough oxygen. When excessive moisture becoming trapped in the center of a mulch pile or bag, the mulch begins to compost; but without enough oxygen, it produces toxic byproducts that dramatically decrease the pH, making it highly acidic. Typically, sour mulch gives off an odor that alerts gardeners to its toxicity, but for whatever reason, the bags we'd bought hadn't. And once a gardener spreads sour mulch on her garden, there is nothing she can do. The toxins leach into the soil and burn the tender roots. It's possible that a more experienced gardener might have forgone mulching altogether as a precaution, but without the telltale sour smell, there was no way I could have known that the mulch was toxic. It was

---

11. "Beware of Toxic Mulch," Cornell gardening resources, Cornell University, last updated October 20, 2015, http://www.gardening.cornell.edu/factsheets/mulch/toxicmulch.html.

frustrating to see my poor young herbs so severely damaged, but I wasn't entirely responsible despite my *feeling* entirely responsible.

Not only does humility free us from the condemnation of others, it also frees us from self-condemnation and unnecessary guilt. Because humility teaches us that our feelings are not the measure of reality, humility also teaches us that the only person who has the right to condemn us is God Himself. In fact, this truth is the larger context of John's assurance that "God is greater than our heart." In writing to believers struggling to have confidence in God's call, John reminds them that their feelings are not the basis of their faith. "By this we shall know that we are of the truth and reassure our heart before him; for whenever our heart condemns us, *God is greater than our heart*, and he knows everything."[12] In other words, the basis of faith is not how you *feel* about your faith but the object of your faith.

One reason that we're tempted to assume unnecessary guilt is because it can make us look humble without actually having to be humbled. We can maintain our place of centrality while still convincing ourselves that we're lowly. But when we navel-gaze or become preoccupied with our weaknesses, we're simply turning our attention back on ourselves; and by judging ourselves, we put ourselves in God's place. We're saying, in effect, that the Holy Spirit is not competent enough to do His work of convicting "the world concerning sin and righteousness and judgment."[13] And if He is not capable, we must do it for Him.

"Do not arrogate to yourself God's own role of apportioning blame and praise, even when the blame lands on your own shoulders. That's a kind of arrogance, too," Ellis Peters writes in *The Virgin in the Ice*, a mystery novel in her Brother Cadfael series

---

12. 1 John 3:19–20.
13. John 16:8.

(who interestingly enough is a twelfth-century monk who tends a physick garden). "It was all too easy to turn honest anxiety . . . into a usurpation of the station of God. To accuse oneself of falling short of infallibility is to arrogate to oneself the godhead."[14]

Or as Hildebrand puts it, "This is precisely the test of true humility, that one no longer presumes to judge whether or not one is too miserable to be included in the call to sanctity but simply answers the merciful love of God by sinking down into adoration."

And this sinking down, this humility, leads to confidence. Hildebrand continues, "The question whether I feel worthy to be called is beside the point; that God has called is the one thing that matters."[15]

Understanding that our emotions are not the measure of God's call may go a long way to closing the confidence gap between men and women. In the May 2014 cover story of the *Atlantic*, journalists Katty Kay and Claire Shipman write about the sociological phenomenon in which men tend to overestimate their abilities while women tend to underestimate theirs, even when controlled evaluations show no difference in competence. Sociologists suggest many causes for the confidence gap—including even chemical differences—but the result of such a gap is that women's self-doubt keeps them from acting, while men's overconfidence leads them to act when they shouldn't.

Of course, this does not mean that all men have an inflated sense of their abilities or that some women couldn't use a dose of humility. But the research does reveal how our emotions don't always correspond with reality. And because they don't, we can't

14. Ellis Peters, *The Virgin in the Ice: The Sixth Chronicle of Brother Cadfael* (New York: Morrow, 1983), 98–99.
15. Dietrich von Hildebrand, *Humility: Wellspring of Virtue* (Manchester, NH: Sophia Institute Press, 1997), 51.

be led by them—especially when it comes to the Holy Spirit's call on our life.

Your belief that God couldn't possibly call you to write or evangelize or advocate for children in foster care means nothing, especially when we're talking about a God who routinely does above and beyond all that we can ask or think. By the same token, your belief that you should preach or plant a church or lead a social media empire means nothing, especially if you lack gifting, experience consistent failure, and are regularly told to seek a different path.

Emotional humility—understanding that God is greater than our heart—solves both these extremes. Humility reminds us that the lack of confidence does not determine whether God has gifted us and called us. Humility also reminds us that the presence of confidence does not mean that God has gifted us and called us. Just because we believe in ourselves doesn't mean we should.[16] Ultimately, by silencing the cacophony of emotion, humility frees you to hear God's call and leads you to a place of both rest and flourishing.

When Nathan saw what had happened to my garden, he drew me aside and assured me that he didn't blame me and so I shouldn't blame myself either. "Don't worry about the money," he said. "This kind of thing happens all the time in gardening. And besides, you know more than you did before, right?" Then he went out and bought seedlings to replace my sad, scorched herbs. He helped me replant them. He also helped me salvage the ones that had survived, stripping them of their dead leaves and promising me that by summer's end, we'd never know the difference.

I didn't know whether to believe him or not.

---

16. In the *Atlantic* article, the authors note the "Dunning-Kruger effect," which is named after the research of psychologists David Dunning and Justin Kruger of Cornell University. The Dunning-Kruger effect is "the tendency for some people to substantially overestimate their abilities. The less competent people are, the more they overestimate their abilities."

By My Spirit

"Not by might, nor by power, but by my Spirit,
says the L<small>ORD</small> *of hosts."* —*Zechariah 4:6*

As much as humility frees us from condemning ourselves, it also frees us from condemning others and using emotion to manipulate them. When you play Holy Spirit in your own life, you'll quickly become comfortable playing Holy Spirit in other people's lives as well. But when you remember that "God is greater than our heart," when you walk in emotional humility, you'll give space for God to do His own work.

One reason we're tempted to manipulate other people's emotions is because it works. We can actually move people to specific actions by stimulating emotional responses in them. In *Rhetoric*, his treatise on effective persuasion, Aristotle points to the power of emotion and recommends "awakening emotion (*pathos*) in the audience so as to induce them to make the judgment desired." For Aristotle, *pathos* should be combined with *ethos* (appeal to morality) and *logos* (appeal to the mind). Working together, these elements engage the whole person; they honor the mind, the emotions, and the moral context in which we find ourselves. But, quite frankly, such robust and ethical argumentation is a lot of work. It's much easier to take shortcuts. It's much easier to simply manipulate people's emotions. Because human beings so readily act on their emotions, all you have to do is stimulate a certain emotional response, and you can lead them wherever you want them to go. This is why politicians stir up fear and greed to convince you to vote for them; it is why advertisers evoke nostalgia or lust to make you buy a soft drink; it why bloggers use shocking phrases in their click-bait titles; and it is why celebrity preachers appeal to guilt and self-righteousness to solicit money.

It is also why we manipulate each other in our churches, friendships, and families.

We don't always recognize what we're doing, in part, because we believe our goals are noble. We want to raise money for a charity or to see someone make a commitment to Christ, so we feel justified in taking shortcuts. We post dehumanizing pictures of impoverished villagers who are desperately waiting for Western help. We pressure seekers to make a decision for Christ "before it's too late." But in so doing, we reveal our pride and destroy the very truth we're trying to promote.

Consider how emotional pressure can undermine the process of coming to faith. When we use fear to persuade a person to make a decision "before it's too late," we make God look like a cosmic bully who is just waiting for the opportunity to strike them down. They may make some kind of commitment or answer an appeal at the end of an event, but at what cost? As soon as the emotional pressure is removed, what will compel them to honor their decision?

Instead, we must forgo emotional manipulation and tell the truth about God's character. The truth is that God is kind and long-suffering toward us, not willing that any should perish,[17] and it is precisely His kindness that makes us run to Him. The truth is that God has waited so long for us, despite our rejection of Him, that we can't help but love Him. And suddenly it is the love of Christ constraining us, not guilt or fear or pressure. Suddenly the Holy Spirit is doing His own work of testifying to the glory of Christ. Suddenly the gospel is changing a person.

This approach is something of what Paul is describing when he writes that he did not preach with "lofty speech or wisdom." Instead of relying on his ability to convince or persuade people, he determines "to know nothing . . . except Jesus Christ and him

---

17. 2 Peter 3:9.

crucified . . . And my speech and my message were not in plausible words of wisdom but in demonstration of the Spirit and of power, so that your faith might not rest in the wisdom of men but in the power of God."[18]

In other words, Paul didn't want people to make decisions based on his personality or persuasiveness; he wanted them to be convinced by the power of God. But this meant that Paul had to trust the power of God himself. He had to humble himself to be nothing more than a mouthpiece. He had to wait on the Holy Spirit to change hearts.

And this is precisely what humility teaches us as well. Humility teaches us that we must pray and speak truth and love, but must not nag and pressure and guilt and manipulate. Humility teaches us to trust God. And suddenly a burden rolls off our back. We are no longer responsible to produce faith in another person's heart. (As if we ever could.) We are no longer responsible for someone's relationship with Christ. We are no longer responsible for the Holy Spirit's work. He is.

My Portion Forever

"To preserve Sweet, Pot, and Medicinal herbs and flowers,
they should be gathered when in bloom, thoroughly dried and
put up in tight boxes or jars, till wanted for use."
—*The Shaker Book of the Garden, 1843*

By summer's end, Nathan's prediction proved correct. My garden healed. The basil leafed out into a bush; the cilantro grew and eventually went to seed; both varieties of parsley produced more than I could ever use. What began so disastrously turned into a

---

18. 1 Corinthians 2:1–5.

garden of plenty. We made mint jelly, dried oregano for the winter, and slipped sprigs of lavender between the sheets in the linen closet. No longer a source of judgment, these herbs—sometimes sweet, sometimes bitter—became a source of beauty and blessing.

So, too, when humility frees us from the oppression of our emotions, when we finally learn that "God is greater than our heart," it also frees us to enjoy the depth and variety of our inner life. We are free to enter into our emotions, letting them do what God intends for them to do: draw us back to Himself.

Because our emotions are powerful, it's tempting to simply shut them down or deny them like the ancient Stoics would. We know the danger that comes when we are led by them, how easily we lash out in anger or manipulate others. But simply controlling our emotions doesn't make us humble, or healthy, people. Instead, humility calls us to something better. Humility calls us to feel deeply precisely because we know that "God is greater than our hearts."

Because "God is greater than your heart," you can trust Him to care for you when your heart breaks through disappointment or suffering. Because "God is greater than your heart," you can trust Him to rejoice with you in times of joy and success. Because "God is greater than your heart," you can trust Him to correct and lead you through doubt and fear. Because "God is greater than your heart," He can handle the depth of your emotions. He is not afraid of them, and as you bring them back to Him, you shouldn't be afraid of them either. In this sense, humility does not shut down your inner life; humility redeems it.

So that, with the psalmist, we can finally and confidently proclaim, "My flesh and my heart may fail, but God is the strength of my heart and my portion forever."[19]

---

19. Psalm 73:26.

FIGURE 7

Tomato, *Solanum lycopersicum*

Chapter 7

Vine-Ripened

"Half of what we are going to teach you is wrong, and half of it is right. Our problem is that we don't know which half is which." —Dr. Charles Sidney Burwell[1]

It happens every year. Every year, I know it's coming, but every year, I'm duped.

It usually happens in the middle of October. And really, it's innocent enough. After a summer of abundance, I've grown accustomed to fresh fruits and vegetables, to their intense colors and variety and depth of flavors, to the ease of strolling out my kitchen door with an empty bowl and returning with it full. So that by the time October rolls around and the garden has finally petered out, I myself am ripe for the picking.

It usually happens when I'm wandering through the produce section of our local grocery store. I see these small, red orbs that look familiar. They look like the small, red orbs I've been picking for the last several months. So I buy them and I take them home and I wash them and I slice them, and with the first bite, I repent. I repent of the foolishness that believed a store-bought tomato

---

1. While variations of this quote exist, Harvard Medical School attributes it to Dr. Burwell during his tenure as dean from 1935–1945, https://hms.harvard.edu/about-hms/facts/past-deans-faculty-medicine.

could ever compare with one ripened on the vine.

Since they were first domesticated, tomatoes (*Solanum lycopersicum*) have been a staple of backyard gardens and sun porches. Grown in pots, on cages, and even over pergolas, a sun-ripened tomato is one of God's clearest acts of common grace. This versatile fruit finds its way into sauces, salads, soups, breads, jellies, and even drinks. Like many home gardeners (nine out of ten if estimates are to be believed), Nathan and I are committed tomato growers. Summer would not be summer without a freshly sliced tomato, still warm from the sun, slathered with mayonnaise and pressed between two pieces of white bread. Summer would not be summer without a pot of tomato soup simmering on the stove waiting to be canned. Summer would not be summer without children's cheeks packed full of cherry tomatoes, giggles and seeds escaping from between their lips.

But in order for summer to be summer, it must begin in late February. While the ground is still cold and the skies a dirty gray, my husband pulls out his seed pack, fills plastic trays with potting soil, and begins the work of growing tomatoes. After he's pressed a tiny seed into each compartment, he places the trays on a rack near our wood stove and rigs up growing lamps to mimic day and night. For the next two months, he watches them closely, watering them and worrying over them like an expectant father. But soon the seeds sprout and tiny tomato plants push their green heads through the soil. By April, they'll have grown six inches; some may even have small yellow blossoms.

At this point, Nathan begins the process of hardening or gradually exposing the seedlings to the elements to prepare them for transplanting. Without hardening, these tender plants will wilt and die once they're put into the ground. So each morning, he carries the trays outside, and each night, he carries them back into the safety of our basement.

"You know," I say to him one day, "it's like you're taking a preschool class to the park. You load them up and let them play outside and then load them up again and bring them back home. Do you think they enjoy it?"

He replies by rolling his eyes and shaking his head. Exactly as he should.

After ten to fourteen days of hardening, the plants are ready to be transplanted in the garden. If all goes well, they'll grow stronger and climb the cages. If all goes well, the yellow blossoms will morph into hard, green globes. If all goes well, we'll have ripe tomatoes by early July.

But somehow, standing in the grocery store in mid-October, I forget all this. I forget that the small, red fruit neatly arranged in towers or packaged in plastic shells are not really tomatoes at all. At least, how I know tomatoes. I forget that these are impostors— bred for long truck rides and perfectly formed shoulders and then gassed to turn their skins red. I forget the difference between what is real and what is fake.

And as a result, I reap disappointment, a mealy, flavorless mouthful of regret.

The Fear of the Lord

"Knowledge is knowing that a tomato is a fruit; wisdom is not putting it in a fruit salad." —Miles Kington

Learning the difference between what is real and what is fake doesn't only apply to tomatoes. In some sense, all of life is a process of choosing between what is true and what is false. The book of Proverbs calls the ability to do this "wisdom." And as you might have guessed, wisdom is ultimately an outgrowth of humility. Becoming wise people, becoming people who can make good decisions only comes when we understand who God is and who we are as a result.

This is why the book of Proverbs opens with a call to humility. The book's main goal is to help the reader "know wisdom and instruction,"[2] but before dispensing any bits of practical advice, Proverbs reminds us that becoming wise starts by learning to fear the Lord. "The fear of the LORD is the beginning of knowledge," Proverbs 1:7 promises, but "fools despise wisdom and instruction."

The word "fool" might hit your ear a bit harshly, but throughout Proverbs, "fool" simply describes a person who makes bad life choices. She makes bad choices about money. She makes bad choices in relationships. She makes bad choices in her work. And she does so for one prevailing reason: She is proud.

At some level, this definition of foolishness is difficult to accept because we tend to associate the ability to make good decisions with the accumulation of knowledge. We tend to believe that coming to a good decision is simply a matter of collecting the right data and processing it mentally. So we rely on "expert" advice (whether that advice comes from a PhD or lifestyle blogger), and the more facts we gather, the more confident we become. But the Scripture roots wisdom in something else entirely; the Scripture roots wisdom in submitting to God. In this sense, a fool is not unwise because she does not have enough facts; she is unwise because she doesn't submit to the source of wisdom Himself.

This is why very educated people can also be very unwise people and why very religious people can be as well. Wisdom is not the result of formal education or religious practice; wisdom is the result of humility. When we remember who we are and who God is, we will also remember where knowledge comes from and we will seek His help to assimilate the facts we've accumulated.

---

2. Proverbs 1:2.

But when the fool rejects God, when she believes she doesn't need God's help, she cuts herself off from the only channel available to her to make good decisions. She becomes trapped by her own experience and her own ability to think through an issue. The problem with this, of course, is that our experience will always feel like it is enough. Our insight will always seem accurate because we simply cannot know what we don't know. A fool's confidence in her own perspective is also why she doesn't receive instruction—from God or other people. She doesn't receive instruction because she doesn't believe she needs it. She's not intentionally rejecting insight. She's not intentionally embracing ignorance. She just thinks she's fine. She's satisfied with her own mind.

Humility, on the other hand, predisposes us to believe that we always have something to learn. Because humility reminds us of our dependency and limitations, it also reminds us of the limits of our mind. It reminds us that there is always a place where our vision could be corrected or our understanding grow. This is why Proverbs 18:15 says, "An intelligent heart acquires knowledge, and the ear of the wise seeks knowledge." The humble person seeks knowledge because the humble person knows how much she doesn't know. The humble person recognizes that she "lacks wisdom" and so she is not afraid to "ask God, who gives generously to all without reproach."[3] And in so doing, she becomes wiser still.

Limits of Knowledge

"O the depth of the riches both of the wisdom and knowledge of God! how unsearchable are his judgments, and his ways past finding out!" —Romans 11:33 (KJV)

---

3. James 1:5.

In the late 1800s, the Supreme Court of the United States heard a case that established precedent for years to come. The case was the result of Edward L. Hedden, the collector of the Port of New York, trying to recoup back taxes from the Nix brothers for produce they had imported from the West Indies. The case hinged on a profound and essential question: *Is the tomato a fruit or a vegetable?*

At one level, picturing the highest court in the land arguing over the nature of tomatoes is nothing short of delightful. Because the New York Port Authority classified tomatoes as vegetables, they were subject to a 10 percent import tax. The Nix brothers argued that tomatoes were fruit and therefore exempt. So lawyers for both sides read from dictionaries and debated the difference between a fruit and vegetable. Scientifically speaking, the tomato is a fruit, which Justice Horace Gray noted is "the seed of plants, or that part of plants which contains the seed, and especially the juicy, pulpy products of certain plants, covering and containing the seed."[4] But in common usage, the tomato is understood as a vegetable because it is served during the main course of a meal.

As much fun as it is to imagine this scene—complete with robed justices, erudite lawyers, piles of books and dictionaries, passionate debate, and intrepid logic all brought to bear on the humble tomato—this case illustrates why humility is essential to our pursuit of knowledge. In trying to answer the question, "Is a tomato a fruit or vegetable?" the court was caught between competing definitions and systems of classification. The overlap of the US tax code, biology, and common usage created a situation in which it was impossible to completely satisfy all of them at the same time. If a tomato is a vegetable, then it can't be a fruit. But if biology says it's a fruit, then it can't be a vegetable. Ultimately, the justices ruled in favor of the Port Authority, prioritizing the

---

4. *Nix v. Hedden*, 149 U.S. 304 (1893).

common use of the term vegetable but only at the loss of scientific accuracy.

And suddenly the limits of our mental categories and our ability to process ideas becomes even clearer. Not only does humility teach us that knowledge comes from outside us, it also reminds us that we cannot perfectly categorize and process the knowledge that we do have. Humility teaches us the limits of human reason.

Learning to embrace the limits of human reason is especially important for those of us raised in the shadow of modernism. In his book *Deep Church*, pastor and author Jim Belcher defines modernism as "a worldview that rejects transcendent truth, instead finding meaning in reason and the solitary individual."[5] In other words, modernism rejects divine revelation and centers knowledge in the human mind. And while modernism finds its roots in the Enlightenment of the seventeenth century, its emphasis on human reason has profoundly shaped Western culture, from the founding of the United States to the persistent false dichotomy between science and religion.

Thomas Jefferson, the great statesman and naturalist, was himself deeply affected by the Enlightenment, and included such rationalist language in his writings as "all men are created equal," after all, not because Scripture reveals us to be, but because such "truths [are] self-evident." In other words, "Any thinking human being can see what I'm saying is true."[6] For men like Jefferson, reaching truth was simply a matter of perfecting the human capacity to observe, argue, and reason. But what modernism fails to account for is the possibility that our minds might be limited and

---

5. Jim Belcher, *Deep Church: A Third Way Beyond Emerging and Traditional* (Downers Grove, IL: IVP Books, 2009), 73.

6. Apparently King George III of England did not see Jefferson's argument as self-evidential and proceeded to "debate" such truths throughout the course of the Revolutionary War.

our reason corrupted by sin. What modernism fails to account for is a God whose "ways are past finding out."

The Right Way

As much as Western thought has been shaped by modernism, Western Christianity has been as well. Our love of human reason and rationality takes several different forms, but it can include proof-texting, confusing principle and application, and relying on apologetics to produce faith. It can look something like:

- If I just teach my children the right answers, they will become believers.
- If I just do enough research, I can find the one "biblical" position on finances, food, entertainment, clothing, schooling, etc.
- If I just confront the logical flaws in my atheist friend's reasoning, I can definitively prove the existence of God, and she will come to faith.
- If I just study long enough, I can finally figure out the hidden meaning of an obscure verse that will unlock the entire Bible.

In each case, "right"ness comes through more and better knowledge. And so we must commit ourselves to the tireless pursuit of knowing. We research and gather facts and peek around every corner for the "real" answer. We become suspicious and never take anything at face value because the stakes are simply too high. *What if we get duped?*

But as Belcher points out in *Deep Church*, the Christian faith is not based on our ability to reason. "We walk by faith in the truth of revelation rather than by indubitable foundations. We follow

Augustine [in saying] 'I believe in order that I might understand.'"[7]
By referring to Augustine, Belcher is not advocating belief apart
from reason; he's advocating "epistemological humility"—accepting that our minds are limited.[8] It's not that truth doesn't exist. It's
not even that human beings can't know truth. Humility simply
leaves room that my understanding of a situation could be wrong.
Perhaps I don't have all the facts; perhaps I've been influenced by
my cultural presuppositions to believe that a tomato is a vegetable; or perhaps I'm simply a limited human being. And because I
am, my faith cannot rest on my own knowledge. My faith cannot
rest on my ability to understand.

In other words, epistemological humility leaves room for grace.

Ultimately our need to be "right" and to defend our "right"eous-
ness is a form of self-reliance and pride. Within this frame, God
approves of us, not based on Christ's merit, but based on our ability to reach the "right" conclusions, to know the "right" answers.
But don't be mistaken, such rational legalists are not all dour-
faced Puritans, desperately trying to squelch your fun. Rational
legalism is not bound by church tradition or side of the aisle. It is
entirely possible to hold very progressive views and hold them out
of the pride of being right. After all, you're not like those back-
ward fundamentalists; you are "enlightened."

In his classic work *The Improvement of the Mind*, seventeenth-century pastor and hymn writer Isaac Watts describes a
person with such a "dogmatical spirit" and notes that it

leads to arrogance of mind. . . . Every one of his opinions appears
to him written as it were with sun-beams; and he grows angry

---

7. Jim Belcher, *Deep Church*, 84.
8. Epistemology is the branch of philosophy concerned with human knowledge, including
what we can and can't know.

that his neighbour does not see it in the same light . . . he tells them boldly, that they resist the truth, and sin against their consciences.[9]

In other words, in order to prove himself "right," the dogmatic man must prove everyone else wrong. And heaven help him, if he ever comes up against his own mistakes. If God's favor rests on him because he is "right"eous, he cannot possibly risk being wrong. He cannot possibly risk an apology. He cannot possibly risk confessing his faults to another person. Watts continues,

> Having asserted his former opinions in a most confident manner, he is tempted now to wink a little against the truth, or to prevaricate . . . lest, by admitting conviction, he should . . . [confess] his former folly and mistake; and he has not humility enough for that.[10]

When we believe our righteousness comes from having the "right" opinions or taking the "right" position on an issue, we can never move from that position. And so, like an animal backed into a corner, we fight and scrap and lash out against anyone who would try to make us. And as James predicts, this kind of rational pride—this "earthly wisdom"—ultimately leads to anxiety and disunity:

---

9. Isaac Watts, *The Improvement of the Mind, Or, A Supplement to the Art of Logic: Containing a Variety of Remarks and Rules for the Attainment and Communication of Useful Knowledge in Religion, in the Sciences, and in Common Life; to Which Is Added, a Discourse on the Education of Children and Youth* (Morgan, PA: Soli Deo Gloria Publications, 1998), 13.
10. Ibid.

If you have bitter jealousy and selfish ambition in your hearts, do not boast and be false to the truth. This is not the wisdom that comes down from above, but is earthly, unspiritual, demonic. For where jealousy and selfish ambition exist, there will be disorder and every vile practice.[11]

If God accepts us based on our being right about every issue, then we must fight to prove ourselves right; but if God accepts us based on our being right, then none of us have any hope. *If, however, God accepts you based on Jesus' being right, then you are safe.*

You are safe in the one who is truth Himself. And, when you are safe, suddenly you can open yourself up to the possibility that you might not know everything. You can open yourself up to the possibility that you never will. And then you can finally rest. Your mind can be at ease. You don't have to worry and fret and stay up late searching out every possible detail before you make a decision. You don't have to be an expert in medicine or education or theology. You don't have to perfectly parse every scriptural text. You don't have to point out where other people are wrong.

"But the wisdom from above," James continues "is first pure, then peaceable, gentle, open to reason, full of mercy and good fruits, impartial and sincere."[12] When you are safe, you can stop fighting. Not because your own mind has made you safe, but because Jesus—the wisdom from above—has made you safe. Is it any wonder, then, that the same Isaac Watts who warns us against trusting in our own minds also penned this refrain?

---

11. James 3:14–16.
12. James 3:17.

When I survey the wondrous cross
On which the Prince of glory died,
My richest gain I count but loss,
And pour contempt on all my pride.[13]

Ripened on the Vine

"With sweetness and tartness playing off each other perfectly,
and juices that burst into your mouth . . . a real tomato's
taste is the distilled essence of sun, warm soil, and
fine summer days." —Barry Estabrook

In his book *Tomatoland*, food journalist Barry Estabrook chronicles the state of the US tomato industry, including why supermarket tomatoes have lost both flavor and nutritional value over the last fifty years.[14] Estabrook notes that to ensure tomatoes can withstand days and weeks in transit, industrial breeders have prioritized toughness over flavor. What flavor tomatoes do have can also be damaged through "chilling injury," a phenomenon that occurs when tomatoes are kept cold in storage. (If you've ever put a ripe tomato in your refrigerator at home, only to remove a soggy, bland mass the next day, you'll know how cold ruins a tomato's flavor.) But the most significant factor contributing to lack of flavor is that tomatoes are actually harvested green. They are picked hard, without the slightest hint of pink. To achieve the necessary hue, they are then gassed with ethylene, which causes the skin to turn red and induces ripening.

In nature, red skin signals that a tomato is ripe. But this is not

---

13. Watts's hymn "When I Survey the Wondrous Cross" was first published in *Hymns and Spiritual Songs* in 1707.
14. Barry Estabrook, *Tomatoland: How Modern Industrial Agriculture Destroyed Our Most Alluring Fruit* (Kansas City: Andrews McMeel Publishing, 2011).

necessarily true of tomatoes that have been forced to turn red. It is entirely possible, and likely, that we are purchasing and consuming unripe fruit. And there would be little way of knowing it until we take the first bite. "Reasonably fresh tomatoes have all but disappeared," journalist Thomas Whiteside noted as early as 1977. "In their place is something that is called a tomato, that has the shape of a tomato and a tinge of the color of a tomato, and that sells at fancy-tomato prices, but serious doubts have been raised about whether it tastes like a tomato."[15]

The dilemma of the store-bought tomato provides insight to how humility creates space for ideas and knowledge to ripen over time. Not only does humility teach us the source and limits of our knowledge, humility also teaches us how to engage the process of learning. Humility teaches us to forgo prepackaged, cellophane wrapped, artificially ripened answers to allow faith to develop naturally.

In other words, humility teaches us to be less concerned with knowing the answers and more concerned with *learning* the answers.

To be fair, part of the reason that growers gas tomatoes with ethylene is because this is what the market demands. As consumers, we want to eat fresh tomatoes both in and out of season. We want to walk into our local grocery store any time of the day, any day of the week, and pick up a red tomato. We want the certainty of knowing that a tomato is always within reach.

In much the same way, we want the certainty of knowing that the answers to life's questions are always within reach. When a problem or choice presents itself, we don't want go through the growing process; we want an answer immediately. So just like we're content with mealy, prepackaged tomatoes because they're easy

---

15. Thomas Whiteside, "Tomatoes," *The New Yorker*, January 24, 1977, 36.

and readily available, we're also content with mealy, prepackaged answers because they're easy and readily available. But humility teaches us a better way. Humility teaches us to wait for God for answers. Humility teaches us to let knowledge ripen on the vine.

In the hours immediately before His death, Jesus spent time teaching and praying with His disciples, reminding them that they must abide in Him in order to bear fruit. He also promises to send the Helper, or the Holy Spirit, to enable them to learn and grow. Jesus promises them, "I still have many things to say to you, but you cannot bear them now. When the Spirit of truth comes, he will guide you into all the truth."[16]

It's interesting that while Jesus is concerned that His disciples grow in their understanding, He is also comfortable with them not knowing all things—in part because they aren't ready for more knowledge yet. Jesus is also confident in the Holy Spirit's ability to take them through the process. But as He told them a few moments earlier, this process can only happen in relationship; it can only happen as they depend on Him; it can only happen as they are connected to Him, the Vine.

In many ways, Jesus' words echo Proverbs 3: "Trust in the LORD with all your heart, and do not lean on your own understanding. In all your ways acknowledge him, and he will make straight your paths." He will guide you into all truth. He will make straight your paths. In God's wisdom the very process of learning binds us to Him in a way that simply knowing the answers cannot. And so He asks you to trust Him. He asks you to live in dependence. He asks you to humble yourself to wait for Him.

This fact that understanding grows over time is particularly significant for those of us who disciple other people—whether we are parents, teachers, pastors, mentors, or friends. We must learn

16. John 16:12–13.

to view spiritual formation as the process of ripening on the vine, not simply the process of turning red. One reason so many people who've grown up in the church seem so immature—so green—is because their faith has not been given space and time to mature naturally. When we are fixated on the goal of "red" tomatoes, we are tempted to prioritize hearing certain phrases or seeing certain religious practice. When questions come, we offer prepackaged, simplistic answers, and unwittingly teach others to find answers this way themselves.

But the world is a complicated, nuanced, unpredictable place, and easy answers aren't sustainable. In fact, the world is so mixed-up and broken, so complicated, that the only one who can lead us through it is God Himself. And so we must teach our children to seek Him. Instead of seeking certainty, we must teach them to follow Jesus in the midst of uncertainty. This doesn't mean neglecting their spiritual ABCs—Bible knowledge, prayer, and community—but it does mean that we must be comfortable with the process of development. We must create space for the questions and doubt that lead to growth.

But to do this, we must be comfortable with questions and un-certainty ourselves. Another reason growers pick tomatoes green is because it seemingly reduces risk. The longer a tomato remains on the vine, the more potential there is for it to contract a disease, be-come a tasty snack for a bird or bugs, or get jostled and break loose. By picking it green, we could think that we're mitigating these risks; but by picking it green, we also ensure that it won't ripen. And so we must become comfortable with the ripening process. We must learn to wait. We must learn to trust. We must remember that we are merely undergardeners. We must remember that the Master Gardener faithfully tends His seedlings and young fruit.

And we must remember that He is growing all of us in the process.

Stewed Tomatoes

"Tomato or Love Apple—This is a very healthy vegetable, and a great favorite when we become accustomed to it, though generally not very palatable at first." —The Shaker Gardener's Manual

When I was young, my grandma made a dish she called simply "stewed tomatoes." It still shows up occasionally at our church suppers, typically in a harvest gold casserole dish. In many ways, stewed tomatoes is the mountain equivalent to convenience food. The recipe calls for only four ingredients: canned tomatoes, butter, sugar, and white bread. All you have to do is pop open a jar of canned tomatoes, stew them with some butter and sugar, and then drop in bits of bread. By the time it reaches the table, it will be a sweet bowl of tomato heaven, summer preserved.

I'd always known that stewed tomatoes was the kind of recipe handed down from generation to generation, but I didn't know exactly how many generations until I stumbled across a similar recipe in a gardening manual published by the United Society of Shakers. At the time of publication, tomatoes had been newly introduced to the American table and homemakers and cooks were still learning how to prepare them. Under Chapter XI: RECIPES FOR COOKERY, &c., the United Society suggests the following preparation for tomatoes:

> Take them when ripe and red, dip them in scalding water, and take off all the skin, cut in quarters and scrape out the seeds; then put them in a clean stew pan and let them simmer about fifteen minutes, then put in a little butter and pepper, stir them a few minutes and they are done. Some prefer some crumbs of wheat bread or grated crackers.

The manual was published in 1843. If I were to write out this recipe for my daughter today, it might look like this:

Grandma Stella's Stewed Tomatoes
Ingredients: canned tomatoes, butter, sugar, white bread
Cook time: 15 minutes
Prep time: 175 years

Tomatoes, it seems, were never meant to be rushed—on the vine or in the stew pot. So, too, humility teaches us to wait. To wait for the Holy Spirit to guide us into all truth. To wait for those we love to come to understanding. To wait for answers that, in God's own wisdom, may never come. But humility also teaches us that we don't need to know everything as long as we know the one who does know.

"Listen diligently to me, and eat what is good, and delight yourselves in rich food," the Lord says through Isaiah. "Incline your ear, and come to me; hear, that your soul may live. . . . For my thoughts are not your thoughts, neither are your ways my ways, declares the LORD. For as the heavens are higher than the earth, so are my ways higher than your ways and my thoughts than your thoughts."[17]

And in this knowledge—in knowing Him—we can finally rest.

---

17. Isaiah 55:2–3, 8–9.

III

He is like a tree planted by streams of
water that yields its fruit in its season,
and its leaf does not wither.
In all that he does, he prospers.

—PSALM 1:3

FIGURE 8

Milkweed, *Asclepias syriaca*

Chapter 8

Natural Resources

"The mountains are calling and I must go."
—*John Muir*

Spring comes late to these mountains, a halting waltz of two steps forward, one step back. The forsythia and crocus are the first to signal its coming, but you can't really trust it until after the last frost. But then the trees leaf out and the forest floor comes alive with ramps, fiddlehead ferns, and wildflowers. One year, after a particularly greedy winter had consumed more than the allotted snow days, the County scheduled school to be in session on Memorial Day. But after a hard winter, the last place anyone wants to be is in a classroom.

"What do you think about letting the kids stay home tomorrow?" Nathan asked me the Sunday before.

"You know what I think."

It was true: He knows that I'm a follow-the-rules, get-the-gold-star, make-the-honor-roll kind of girl. He, on the other hand, made it through school believing that grades are an exercise in averages, demerits are to be budgeted, and asking forgiveness is always easier than asking permission.

"I just thought we could meet Mom and Dad at Smart View. We haven't been hiking yet this spring."

Smart View Trail sits just off the Blue Ridge Parkway at mile marker 154, a little under an hour from where we live. And it was true that we hadn't gotten out much that spring—our weeks filled with school, our weekends with church.

"I dunno." I balked. "I don't want to disrupt the teachers' plans."

"C'mon," he wheedled, "the only reason the teachers are going tomorrow is because they have to. Sue told me yesterday that she's not making her own kids go and she works for the school."

This also was true. The County may set the calendar, but in my experience, our small community operates on an unspoken understanding. Hunting season corresponds with a surprisingly high rate of "appointments," and snow makeup days are less than productive.

"Think of it this way," he continued. "We're actually making less work for them. Three fewer students to worry about."

So the next morning found us tramping a dirt path through a fresh, spring forest, the children running fifty to a hundred yards ahead learning more than they would miss. For about an hour, we followed the three-mile loop along a cascading stream, across a log bridge, and up and down the ridge. Sunlight filtered down through the leafy canopy while we paused every so often to examine native rose quartz, delicate lady slippers, and the chubby caterpillars crossing our path. At one point, the trail steepened, and then almost without warning, opened onto an elevated clearing that offered us what could only be described in the local vernacular as "a right smart view" of the mountains in the distance.

The clearing also held an abandoned cabin.

The cabin was in good condition, although the chinking between the rough-hewn logs had long ago crumbled and Virginia creeper grew up the side of the stone chimney. A nearby historical marker informed us that the Trail family had built a cabin on this spot in 1890 and inhabited it until 1925. (A Trail family descendent informed me that they'd still be there if the Parkway hadn't come through.)

In the city, those years would have meant telephones, electric lights, and indoor plumbing, but out here, on a lonely hillside, 1890 could have as easily been 1690. Because of the isolating nature of mountain life, people like the Trails had to be resourceful. To survive, they would have gardened and kept livestock within feet of their front door. They would have made occasional trips to town for things they couldn't grow, but everything else would have been foraged from the natural world around them. Meat, herbs, medicines, and even fibers would have come from the forest we'd just walked through.

One such natural resource—a plant we'd seen earlier that morning—is the common milkweed (*Asclepias syriaca*). Most people know the milkweed by its distinctive seedpod that releases hundreds of soft, downy seeds in the fall. But in the late spring, you can spot the milkweed by its large spherical blossoms that comprise a multitude of tiny star-shaped flowers. These flowers are prime real estate for pollinators like bees and butterflies—the nectar so tempting, in fact, that Native Americans and pioneers used it as a sweetener.

Milkweed gets its name from a sticky white substance that is secreted when the leaves or stalk are damaged. This residue is mildly toxic—just enough to make the insects that feed on it unpalatable to predators and just enough to cure warts in humans. Pioneers used other parts of the milkweed to suppress coughs, fight typhus, and cure dysentery. Despite the toxicity of the sap, the milkweed is also edible; with a little knowledge and proper preparation, you can enjoy the early shoots, immature buds, and even young seedpods. Milkweed floss also came in handy during WWII when the

US government purchased it from foragers to use in life jackets and pillows.

The versatility of the common (or not-so-common) milkweed illustrates how mountain families like the Trails relied on the natural resources around them. Here, all in one plant, was beauty, food, medicine, and textiles. But the milkweed was far from the only plant available to settlers. The forest was full of potential—all of it just waiting to be gleaned by resourceful people.

Most of us do not live like the Trail family did in 1890, but we too are surrounded by an abundance of resources. We have at our disposal both tangible and intangible resources of time, money, talents, intelligence, education, influence, and family. But how we choose to engage these resources will determine whether we thrive or struggle in the world. So how do we engage our own resources with humility? How do we honor these gifts? What would it look like to be "resourceful" people?

Humble Thanks

"We git what we git and we don't throw a fit."
—my son's kindergarten teacher

The first step to engaging our resources with humility is to recognize how much we have been given. This may sound simplistic, but left unchecked, pride blinds us to God's good gifts. Because pride convinces us that we are more significant than we really are, it also convinces us that we deserve a certain experience of the world; and when something disrupts that, our pride reveals itself by complaining.

Children are particularly obvious complainers: They balk at eating unfamiliar foods, throw tantrums at the mere suggestion of putting on their own shoes and socks, and protest that "It (everything) is not fair!" Adults are just as prolific complainers, but we tend to be more subtle about it. One emerging form of adult complaining is the microcomplaint. Related to the humble brag, the microcomplaint highlights small inconveniences as a way to signal superiority. In writing for *The New York Times*, novelist Teddy Wayne describes a typical microcomplainer:

> The offender moans about a lack of free time because of the
> burdensome demands of a hugely successful career. Horrors of
> luxury travel feature prominently. . . . In this way, the microcom-
> plaint functions as a kind of reverse boast: I may be celebrating
> a new job or engagement with a Michelin-starred dinner, but
> look at how much I have suffered today — I'm deserving of more
> attention.[1]

Most of us don't have the opportunity to complain about luxury travel or Michelin-starred dinners, but we still find ways to signal our superiority. We complain about the struggle to be understood by others (superiority of uniqueness). We complain about keeping our new white leather couch clean with young children (superiority of affluence). We complain about how lonely it is to be a leader in ministry (superiority of influence). But as unfounded as our stress may be, we still feel it. In that moment, our complaint feels entirely valid. And it feels valid because we actually believe ourselves worthy of a different experience. We fail to recognize how much we already enjoy because we assume we deserve it or because we've earned it.

We are blind to our own privilege.

In contemporary speech, the word privilege is loaded with

---

1. Teddy Wayne, "My Complaint Box Overfloweth," *New York Times*, November 15, 2015.

connotation: You've probably heard it in conversations about "white privilege," "male privilege," or "first-world privilege." And undoubtedly, behind these conversations lie myriad assumptions, political agendas, and personal experiences. But if you step away from the specific issues, the concept of privilege is pretty non-confrontational. In its most basic sense, privilege is the reality that some people have access to more resources through no effort of their own, and some people have access to fewer resources through no fault of their own. These resources include anything in our environment that we can use to make our way through the world: wealth, social status, intelligence, time, education, and so on.

The problem with privilege is that we rarely see our own. Because we only know our own experience, we rarely recognize how much we have been given and how much those gifts have smoothed our way. We also fail to remember how much we have inherited from past generations.[2] While our grandparents fought oppressive regimes, we're the ones who enjoy freedom. While our parents worked entry-level jobs, we're the ones who enjoy the profit. And yet, we did nothing to arrange the circumstances of our birth or childhood. Naked we came into the world and naked we will return.[3] Paul drives home this point in 1 Corinthians 4:7:

> For who sees anything different in you? What do you have that you did not receive? If then you received it, why do you boast as if you did not receive it?

Humility teaches us that all is gift. Humility teaches us thankfulness. But it is not a thankfulness based in having more than

---

2. In failing to recognize how much previous generations have shaped our own success, we can also fail to see how much generations of poverty and oppression will shape other people as well. While we may inherit blessing, other people inherit hardship.
3. Job 1:21.

other people because that kind of thankfulness fluctuates on whoever you're comparing yourself with. As long as you're looking at people with fewer resources, you will be thankful. But what happens when you meet up with your college friend who earns twice what you do and has traveled the world—all while maintaining wonderfully diverse friendships and an intimate family life? If your thankfulness is rooted in comparison, it will evaporate in an instant.

No, gratitude born from humility is not a gratitude rooted in having more than someone else. It is a gratitude rooted in having anything at all. Instead of comparing what you have with other people (either more or less), humility teaches you to compare what you have now with what you had when you entered this world. You entered this world with nothing. You didn't even have clothing on. Your very existence is a gift and everything that you have or have ever had is a gift as well.

Remembering how we entered the world helps us understand why Jesus calls us to enter His kingdom like babies, why we must be born again. At one point in His earthly ministry, the disciples were arguing about who was greatest in the kingdom—in essence, microcomplaining. Jesus corrects them by saying, "Truly I say to you, unless you turn and become like children, you will never enter the kingdom of heaven."[4] We often associate the call to become like children with a childish innocence—a faith that is untainted by cynicism or suspicion—but Jesus emphasizes something different. Therefore, He continues, "whoever *humbles* himself like this child is the greatest in the kingdom of heaven."[4]

For Jesus, childhood embodies humble dependence. Being born again is not simply a fresh start; the language of childbirth also illustrates how we are to humbly depend on God for life.

4. Matthew 18:3–4.

We are to depend on Him the same way a child depends on his mother for life and nourishment. It's not surprising, then, that this is exactly how Jesus entered our world. Jesus came as an infant—helpless, naked, and vulnerable. He left the riches of heaven to become a child who owned nothing. And by doing so, He reminds us that this is the way we must enter His kingdom as well. Helpless, naked, and vulnerable. But this offends our pride. We like to believe that we are self-made men and women. We like to believe that we possess what we have because of our hard work and intentionality and focus. But we do not. All is gift.

And when we finally learn this—when we finally realize that we have nothing that we have not received—we've taken the first step to becoming grateful, humble people who can steward our resources well.

Ecology of Dependence

"But most of all I shall remember the monarchs, that unhurried westward drift of one small winged form after another, each drawn by some invisible force." —Rachel Carson

Besides being a resource for early pioneers, milkweed is also a resource for many insects, including the iconic monarch butterfly. With over a hundred varieties spread along their migration route, milkweed provides sustenance for the monarch's yearly pilgrimage from Canada to central Mexico—a veritable chain of rest stops along the monarch highway. But milkweed plays an even more important role in the monarch life cycle. Monarchs lay their eggs exclusively on milkweed and their young larva feed off it. Turn over a milkweed leaf in the spring, and there on the underside, you'll see small, light yellow orbs—future butterfly kings and butterfly queens.

But in the last two decades, monarch populations have declined dramatically, leading conservationists to call for their inclusion on the federal list of endangered species. Scientists believe that there are many contributing factors—illegal deforestation and unusual weather patterns—but famed entomologist Lincoln Brower, research professor at Sweet Briar College and student of the monarch for sixty years, points to an additional cause: the loss of milkweed.[5]

Milkweed traditionally grows along roadsides and at the edges of fields and fence rows, so cutting and spraying on the shoulders and medians of highways reduces the number of milkweed. But according to Dr. Brower, the largest single culprit is widespread use of herbicides and genetically modified crops. When herbicides are sprayed over large areas, like fields of corn or soybeans, genetically modified crops resist it; but other plants in the immediate area, including milkweed, die. And when they do, a delicate ecological balance shifts. Suddenly without milkweed, monarchs start to die too.

Just as in nature, our resources are part of a larger ecology. Even after we learn to see our resources as gifts from God, we must then wrestle with the fact that resources are not equally distributed—both as a result of human greed and God's sovereignty. Some people are born geniuses. Some people struggle through school. Some are born among the wealthy top 10 percent.[6] Some are born into an impoverished region, lucky to survive infancy. Some are born into intact nuclear families. Some will never know their fathers.

---

5. Dr. Brower's body of research can be accessed via multiple academic clearinghouses, but this particular observation comes from a January 31, 2014 press release on Sweet Briar College's website at http://www.biologicaldiversity.org/news/press_releases/2014/monarch-butterfly-08-26-2014.html.

6. While most of us are not in the wealthy 1 percent, global economic data indicates that the average American family is well within the top 10 percent of the world's wealthiest people.

Some are born close to power and influence. Some far from it. So how does humility engage such inequity?

First, simply recognizing inequity does not guarantee that we are engaging our resources with humility. It's entirely possible that the same pride that blinds us to our privilege can lead us to feeling guilty about it. We know that we don't deserve more than another person, but we also know that we have more than another person. And so in an attempt to deal with this guilt, we can pursue a form of asceticism, all while keeping ourselves at the center of the conversation.

We may abdicate positions of power, give away extra material goods, and move into smaller homes. But if we do it out of guilt (and make sure to broadcast our sacrifices loudly enough), our experience of the world is still the driving force. And we miss the fact that even the ability to embrace a minimalist lifestyle is based in abundance. As award-winning writer David Brooks observes,

> One of the troublesome things about today's simplicity move-
> ments is that they are often just alternate forms of consumption.
> . . . Early in life you choose your identity by getting things. But
> later in an affluent life you discover or update your identity by
> throwing away what is no longer useful, true and beautiful.[7]

In other words, because we have access to so many resources, we have the luxury of throwing them away without a second thought.

There are, of course, many legitimate reasons to pursue simplicity, including the desire to move through the world less encumbered and to promote ethical consumption. But pursuing simplicity itself does not necessarily make us humble or grateful people. Sometimes all simplicity does is mask our pride and

---

7. David Brooks, "The Evolution of Simplicity," *New York Times*, November 3, 2015.

self-dependence. If we take a great deal of satisfaction in how little we need, in how much we reject abundance, simplicity becomes nothing more than an asceticism that, as theologian J. I. Packer puts it, is "too proud to enjoy the enjoyable."[8]

Instead of rejecting our resources, humility teaches us to receive them as gifts and to use them for God's glory and the good of those around us. Humility teaches us to cultivate the milkweed in our own backyard. One simple way that scientists and advocacy groups are working to preserve the monarch is by encouraging gardeners to cultivate native milkweed around their homes and businesses. Groups like Monarch Watch organize the collection of milkweed seeds and the free distribution of milkweed plugs. The goal is to restore the imbalance by sustainable cultivation. And while such conservation efforts require a high level of organization, careful research, expert oversight, and successful fundraising, for most of us, saving the monarch starts by developing the resources in our own backyards.

Faithful Stewards

"Everyone to whom much was given,
of him much will be required." —Luke 12:48

Jesus once told a story about a lord who goes on a journey and entrusts three servants with his wealth. One of the servants receives five talents, one receives two talents, and one receives one. Just as in real life, there is a disproportionate allotment of resources, and even more interestingly, a disproportionate allotment of talent. The lord distributes the money "each according to his ability." While the lord is away, the first and second servants invest their talents

---

8. J. I. Packer, "The Joy of Ecclesiastes," *Christianity Today*, September 2015, 56.

and double their resources. The third servant, however, buries his one talent and waits for his master's return. So afraid he might lose it, he squirrels it away.[9]

When the lord returns, the first two servants present the profit they have made and receive the same commendation: "Well done, good and faithful servant. You have been faithful over a little; I will set you over much. Enter into the joy of your master." But when the third servant comes groveling to him, making excuses for why he did not develop his resources—even blaming his failure on his master's character!—the lord condemns him and takes his investment back. And the very thing the servant fears happens: He loses his talent, not because he took a risk but precisely because he didn't.

It's striking how similar the acts of burying and planting are. Both involve strenuous work, both require digging a hole in the ground, both place an object into the earth. But despite involving the same physical actions, burying and planting have very different results. When the final servant buried his talent, he was trying to preserve it because he feared he would lose it. In a world of scarcity, we too fear we will lose our resources and so, like him, we "bury" our resources instead of planting them. We cling to our time, wealth, even our family life, unwilling to develop or share them with others. It's not that we aren't busy—we may be very busy digging holes to protect our resources—but if we are trying save them for ourselves, we will have very little to show for our work.

But it is precisely the fact that our resources do not belong to us—that they have been given to us by our good, kind Master—that frees us to take risks. When everything is gift and when we learn to trust the Giver of those gifts, we learn a kind of humility that makes us fearless and productive. And instead of either hoarding or rejecting our resources, we cultivate them. Instead

9. Matthew 25:14–30.

of burying them, we plant them. As Rabbi Joseph Telushkin observes, humility teaches us that

> if we have greater wisdom, then we also have a greater responsibility to bring people to understanding and wisdom. If we have wealth, then we have a greater responsibility to help those in need. If we occupy a position of power, we have greater obligation to help the oppressed.[10]

One of the most distinctive features of milkweed is its seedpod that holds hundreds of seeds. Each milkweed plant will produce several pods, and a large colony of milkweed can contain hundreds of plants. This means hundreds of thousands of seeds. These seeds hold the future for both milkweed and the monarch butterfly. But they do no good inside the pod. They do not become a viable resource until the pod is broken open and the seeds scattered. When we consider our resources, it is not enough to simply count our one thousand gifts. Our one thousand gifts are actually one thousand opportunities: the very means by which God intends to seed His world.

Seeds of Faith

"Who could believe in prophecies . . . that the world would end this summer, while one milkweed with faith matured its seeds?" —Henry David Thoreau

Several years ago, Nathan and I went through a period of financial instability. After a difficult ministry placement, he was unem-

---

10. Joseph Telushkin, *A Code of Jewish Ethics, Volume 1: You Shall Be Holy* (New York: Bell Tower, 2006), 212.

ployed for six months and then underemployed for another year, making nine dollars an hour as a bank teller. He picked up additional work cleaning the bank after hours, but with three children ages six and under, it simply wasn't enough. I tried to find work myself but with limited availability (and a BA in the humanities), even retail stores weren't interested. Despite our best efforts, we ended up on food stamps and Medicaid.

I had never felt more conflicted in my life. Everything in me said that I needed to be "working" because that's what you do. You work hard. You pay your bills. You do what has to be done. (Forget the fact that I was already working by caring for our young children and, at that point, homeschooling the oldest.) But it was during this time that God taught me a significant lesson about stewarding even limited resources.

When it became clear that a degree in the humanities (while having the potential to make one an entertaining dinner guest) would not result in a paid position, I began to wonder what I should do with it. At the same time, our daughter was moving into elementary school, and I had the first glimpse that she would not always be little. One day she would be a woman and what she saw me doing with my life would play a large role in shaping how she understood her own. More than anything, I wanted her to be a woman of humble obedience. A woman who would answer God's call with courage instead of fear. A woman who would make the most of the life she had been given.

So I took a step of faith myself: Cooped up in a nine-hundred square foot, two-bedroom apartment with three small children, I started writing.

I committed to God that I would spend the next two years (the equivalent to earning a master's degree or a skilled technical degree) learning the craft. I didn't know how it would end, but I did know that I had been given a resource and the opportunity to develop it. In His own unpredictable way, God was using the US taxpayer to provide groceries and health care so I could learn to write. Like the servant with two talents, I wasn't responsible for the resources I didn't have; I was responsible for the ones I did have. And what I had was naptime and evenings.

A few years later, after we'd reached a level of financial stability, I faced another, similar challenge. By this time all the children were in school and Nathan was earning a sustainable salary. During the hours of 8:00 to 2:00, Monday through Friday, late August to early June (barring snow days and vacations), I had no demands on my schedule. At first, I felt guilty. I knew other moms who were forced to work outside the home by financial constraints. I knew moms whose days were busy homeschooling or who still had toddlers and infants, or both. But here I was with my hands full of time. But if I had learned anything, it's that privilege comes with responsibility. So I continued writing. I volunteered at our kids' school and invested in our church. I wasn't trying to earn my freedom; I just wanted to use my freedom well. And through the process I resolved the following:

1. I will not overlook my privilege. I will take stock of the resources that God has given me including time, talent, education, and wealth.
2. I will not feel guilty about what God has put in my hands or attempt to earn it. I accept it as a gift and rejoice in it.
3. I will allow God to lead me in cultivating these gifts for His glory and the good of those around me.

You, too, have resources at your disposal. They may not be many or public, but you have them. And no matter how small, no matter how few, God intends for you to use them. He intends for you to become a humble, resourceful person, first by receiving His gifts with gratitude and then by cultivating them for the good of those around you.

But in His wisdom, He's crafted the world in such a way that you can't do this apart from Him. You will regularly have to take risks, you will regularly feel pressed past your abilities, you will regularly feel like the husk of your life is being broken open and your seeds scattered to the wind. But this is exactly how He means to teach you humility. This is exactly how He means to relieve you of your burden of guilt and self-reliance. Just as you must accept your resources as good gifts from Him, you must accept that you cannot cultivate them apart from Him. The very process is meant to teach you dependence.

Healing for the Nations

"Let him labor, doing honest work with his own hands,
so that he may have something to share with anyone in need."
—Paul to the church at Ephesus

When Carl Linneaus, the father of modern taxonomy, first organized his system of classification in the 1700s, he grouped milkweeds under the genus Asclepias, which he named after the *Asclepius*, the Greek god of healing. As much as milkweed is an invaluable source of healing for both humans and butterflies, our thousands of gifts are sources of healing for the nations. The natural resources that you enjoy—time, money, intelligence and abilities, social status, political freedom—all of these gifts have been given to you to "seed" the world with other healing plants.

So instead of asking "Do I deserve this gift?" humility teaches us to ask, "What has God given and what responsibility do I have because of it?" And by doing so, humility changes the frame of reference entirely. Suddenly we are no longer at the center; God is. Suddenly our sense of entitlement or guilt no longer drives our choices. Suddenly everything is a gift and everything has purpose.

FIGURE 9

Green Beans, *Phaseolus vulgaris*

Chapter 9

Field of Dreams

"If you don't want to snap green beans when you grow up,
you'll have to marry a doctor." —my aunt

It was the kind of advice you'd expect from the lips of a character in a Jane Austen novel. The kind of universal truth that testifies to the fact that "a single man in possession of a good fortune must be in want of a wife." Or that "there certainly are not so many men of large fortune in the world as there are pretty women to deserve them."[1] But instead of coming from an Austen novel, this particular bit of wisdom regarding the correlation between doctors and legumes came from my aunt one summer when I was a teenager. We were snapping green beans, and I was grousing about it.

I don't remember what set me to complaining that particular day. Picking, snapping, and processing beans had been synonymous with summer for as long as I could remember: green beans, yellow wax beans, and some years, kidneys and limas. As the heat of July rolled into August, I knew I'd be hunched over rows and rows of beans, my back aching, my hands and arms itching and irritated from brushing against the plants. The dusty earth would

1. The first quotation is from *Pride and Prejudice* (1813), the second from *Mansfield Park* (1814).

filter through my canvas sneakers, and when I wiggled my toes, I felt the grit between them.

Usually the children picked and snapped while my mother canned. After picking, we'd lug our bowls of beans back to the house to sit in the air conditioning or out on the front porch. Some days we were allowed to watch TV while we snapped—if we kept moving, because "the canner's ready and hurry up and get them finished." In the kitchen, freshly sterilized mason jars were waiting for us, lined up on the counter, each with a mound of canning salt in the bottom. In an average year, we would put up sixty or seventy quarts; on a spectacular year, the number would surpass a hundred. Eventually, my mom started freezing some, a process that saved both time and flavor, but she never gave up canning altogether. For one thing, who had a chest freezer that could hold a hundred quarts of green beans?

So the day my aunt offered me this bit of marriage advice, it wasn't a surprise to be elbow-deep in snips and snaps. Maybe my discontent came from having town friends whose summers consisted of league softball and trips to Myrtle Beach. Maybe I was just looking for something to complain about. But even though I don't remember what prompted my aunt's advice, I do remember that it was one of the first times I realized that I could potentially plan my life. It was as simple as this: Don't want to snap green beans? Marry a doctor.

When You Grow Up

"There is a divinity that shapes our ends, rough-hew them how we will." —William Shakespeare, Hamlet

Of course, if you live any length of time, you know that planning the future isn't at all simple. It starts easily enough with questions of "What do you want to be when you grow up?" and childhood dreams and play sets and promises that if you just put your mind to it, "You can be whatever you want to be." But then life becomes complicated. You enter adulthood and don't get accepted to the university you wanted. But you do get into another, and you work hard and get good grades; but because you're also working to pay tuition, they're not as good as you know they could be. Through a lucky break, you land a good job and start looking to take the next steps toward the life you planned—buying a house, getting married, maybe even starting a family. But then your dating relationships always seem to fizzle or you're facing infertility or you get laid off. Maybe the marriage you worked so hard to cultivate crumbles with one late-night confession.

And suddenly the idea that you have any control over your life seems ludicrous. So how does humility speak to our plans? How does humility teach us to navigate desires that are both fulfilled and unfulfilled? How does humility teach us to cast the lot "into the lap" but still believe that "its every decision is from the Lord"?[2]

Again, remember what humility is: Humility is understanding who God is and who we are. Humility remembers both your human limitation and God's transcendent power. And perhaps no other passage better captures the interplay between our plans and God's control over them than Proverbs 16:9: "The heart of man plans his way, but the Lord establishes his steps."

At first glance, the word "but" in this verse appears to signal a strict contrast between "our will" and "God's will." Instead of a contrast, though, this verse is better understood as an observation about increasing levels of sovereignty. The word "but" also carries the idea of "and." There are actually two truths being communicated here:

---

2. Proverbs 16:33.

"The heart of man plans his way"
and
"the LORD establishes his steps."

Made in God's image, human beings have a certain ability (and responsibility) to make decisions. Just a few verses previously in verse 1 of chapter 16, Solomon writes that "the plans of the heart belong to man." Dreaming is the particular purview of the human condition. While animals may gather for the future, they don't imagine changing the future; they are subject to the natural rhythms around them. And God doesn't dream about the future either (at least not the way we think about dreaming) if only because He's guiding it! No, dreaming is something distinct to humans, a privilege of being made in the image of the Creator. But even as we dream, humility teaches us to never lose sight of who's actually in control. We make plans. But only God can make those plans happen. As the old preacher might bellow from the platform of the revival tent, a worn copy of sacred Scripture grasped firmly in hand and raised high: "Man proposes, but God disposes."

For some of us, it's difficult to imagine that we can or even should pursue our dreams and desires. Some of us have been taught to surrender our lives to "whatever God wants." The problem, of course, is that "whatever God wants" is entirely vague—the kind of truism that a lot of people say but few can fully explain. The only thing we know for sure is that "what God wants" must be in opposition to what we want. So to plan anything—even what we think we would like to do or places we'd like to go—seems presumptuous. Who are we to tell God what we want? We, who have such corrupted hearts. We, whose hearts are deceitful and desperately wicked. After all, there are really only two choices in life: You can please God or you can please yourself.

But this dichotomy misses a larger truth. Just as God is the source of your life and gifting, God is also the source of your desires. And through Jesus, He is actively redeeming those desires. He is actively restoring your ability to want the right things in the right way. He is actively giving you a new heart. In this sense, the greater presumption is not found in speaking your desires but failing to acknowledge their existence in the first place. If they do not exist, how can they be reformed? *If they do not exist, how can they be changed?*

In *Teach Us to Want*, a theological reflection on the nature of desire, Jen Pollock Michel writes:

> The simple question, "What do I want?" can lead to important change . . . [but]it's often a truth we'd rather avoid. Our dismissal of desire may be built less on our holy hesitations . . . ignoring our desires may serve as the convenient way we remain ignorant and resist change.[3]

Surprisingly enough, humility teaches us to embrace desire as a means of learning to submit to God. It is precisely through the process of wanting certain things that we also learn to trust God to fulfill those desires or to trust Him when he changes them. It is precisely through the process of learning to plan that we learn to depend on a God who makes our plans happen.

Pride, on the other hand, demands to know God's will before it will act. It balks and halts and refuses to move until success is guaranteed. In other words, sometimes the failure to plan is a form of arrogance that expects knowledge beyond our human capacity to know. When we refuse to plan before we "know," we are asking for the same level of knowledge about our future as God

3. Jen Pollock Michel, *Teach Us to Want: Longing, Ambition & the Life of Faith* (Downers Grove, IL: InterVarsity Press, 2014), 43.

has. But this is not how God works. Instead, to humble us, God only reveals the course of our lives one step at a time. God only makes our path straight before us with each step of faith. God does not offer us a map so much as a promise to guide us on the journey. Speaking through the prophet Isaiah, God reminds His people that though

> the Lord give you the bread of adversity and the water of affliction, yet your Teacher will not hide himself anymore, but your eyes shall see your Teacher. And your ears shall hear a word behind you, saying, "This is the way, walk in it," when you turn to the right or when you turn to the left.[4]

And it is precisely this "slow reveal" that keeps us dependent on Him. It is precisely the process of pursuing our desires and waiting for Him to either establish or alter our plans that humbles us. It is precisely the process of pursuing desire that brings us rest.

What You Want

"The desire is thy prayers; and if thy desire is without ceasing, thy prayer will also be without ceasing. The continuance of your longing is the continuance of your prayer." —Augustine of Hippo

During the season that God led me to begin writing, He simultaneously walked my husband through a process of owning his desires. After a few months of respite, Nathan started the process of searching for a full-time ministry position. It was exhausting. He'd spend hours scrolling through ministry placement websites and ask friends and family to keep their ears open. Already dis-

---

4. Isaiah 30:20–21.

placed from the communities where we'd both grown up, he threw a pretty wide net. He told everyone, "I'm willing to go anywhere and do anything God wants me to." And he meant it.

A position as an assistant pastor? I can do that.

A church in a metro area? Sure, why not.

A children's pastor? I have three kids already, what's a few more?

The truth was that my husband was all but directionless. He had enough positive feedback to keep him pursuing church work, but it wasn't much more than a breadcrumb trail. As the search dragged on and responses started to come in more slowly, we began to feel desperate. This was not working out the way we'd planned. The apartment was feeling smaller than its nine hundred square feet. Winter was coming again. There were no savings.

At a particularly low point, when we finally had nothing to lose, when we'd finally hit the bottom, I looked at him and said with exasperation, "I wish you'd stop talking about what 'God wants'—what do you want?!" (I'm a good wife like that.)

He paused and clenched his jaw the way he does when he's trying to decide whether he can say what he's really thinking. Then he dropped his head and his voice became quiet, almost a whisper.

"I—I just want to be a country pastor in Virginia."

"Well, then, for heaven's sake," I said, throwing my arms in the air, "let's just do that."

For heaven's sake. For the good of the kingdom. Let's just do that.

Part of submitting to God also means recognizing that even our desires originate from Him. As much as you cannot make yourself or orchestrate the events of your life or shape your unique personality, you can no more create the desires of your heart. Like the lump of clay on the potter's wheel, we cannot ask, "Why have you made me like this?"[5] We must simply accept how we have been made.

It is entirely possible, of course, that even our God-given desires are out of alignment. It is entirely possible that Nathan's desire to be a country pastor could have been corrupted. He could have been motivated by the need to be a big fish in a small pond. He could have been motivated by fear of another, less familiar context. He could have been motivated by a need to be needed.

Or.

Or God could be at work in his life. And if God was at work in his life, then his desire to be a country pastor could also have been the natural result of his gifting, temperament, and background. It could be the result of having grown up in a small, country church, and knowing almost instinctively its rhythms and rituals. It could be the result of our unique combination of gifting. It could be the result of a man who loves to garden and just wanted to go home to Virginia. It could be the result of everything God had already been doing in his life for the last thirty years. Ultimately, when you acknowledge your desires and risk owning them, you are agreeing with God about who He has made you to be. You are relinquishing control. You are no longer reserving an option on your future, believing that you can make yourself whoever you want to be. By acknowledging your desires, you are embracing the truth that God has made you to be something very particular.

And, ultimately, this leads to rest. When you recognize that you love something and are gifted to do it, you must also immediately recognize that you do not love everything, and you are not gifted to do everything. Suddenly you realize your own limitations; desire humbles you. And suddenly you are free from the tyranny of "keeping your options open." You are free from the

---

5. Romans 9:20.

responsibility of feeling like you have to "do it all." You are free to do only what you have been made to do. As art professor, wife, and mother, Michelle Radford shared with me, when she owned her specific calling, it set her free to throw her energy at the roles and relationships God is specifically holding her responsible for. Though this may seem somewhat inconsequential, it has slowed down the mental traffic in my brain and put my soul at ease. I can use all that saved energy to love and serve others through my own legitimate vocations rather than complicate the work others are trying do. All the while I am growing in my trust in the One who superintends all vocations.

Lord Willing

"The lot is cast into the lap, but its every decision is from the LORD." —Proverbs 16:33

Fast-forward from that sweaty summer when my aunt first advised me to marry a doctor and you know that I didn't. And while correlation is not causation, it is also an undeniable fact that I still pick and snap green beans every year. One spring, shortly after we'd settled back in Virginia, Nathan came home from visiting his parents with a plastic zipper bag of dried beans.

"Did your mom send these for dinner?" I asked innocently enough, picking the bag up to examine it more closely. My in-laws have been homesteading for over forty years, and they often send fruits and vegetables, cut flowers, and even fresh sausage home with him.

"Oh no," he exclaimed, grabbing the bag from me. "These are Mrs. Clovis Richards' beans." There are moments in every marriage when the trust you've built over the years is the only thing that allows you to continue a conversation on the assumption that it will eventually make sense. This was one such moment.

"Mrs. Clovis Richards' beans?"

"Well, they're actually Dad's beans but he got them from Ida Mae Belcher who got them from Mrs. Richards who went to our church when I was growing up. Dad says they have a good flavor and produce well so I want to grow them this year." Apparently, the small white beans that Nathan was now protectively clutching to his chest had been circulated and passed down from generation to generation in the small community where he grew up. Mrs. Richards herself had passed away a few years ago at the age of ninety, but her beans lived on. My father-in-law had been growing them for about fifteen years; and each year, after harvesting most of the beans, he'd make sure to let enough go to seed so he could propagate them again the following year.

Unlike the bush beans I'd grown up with, Mrs. Clovis Richards' beans were pole beans (*Phaseolus vulgaris*), which means they climb like Jack's magic beanstalk. And so during the next week, my husband constructed four bamboo trellises and planted Mrs. Clovis Richards' beans at the base. Within a few days, the beans had spouted and were climbing the trellises just as they should. Within a few weeks, they had blossomed, and we knew that fresh beans were within our grasp. But then nothing happened. Or, at least, very little happened. A few beans developed but nothing near the quantity my father-in-law had described and by no means enough to put up for the winter. If we were lucky, we might get enough for a meal. It was puzzling, but any number of factors could explain it. Maybe Mrs. Clovis Richards' beans preferred a higher altitude; maybe our soil was different from my father-in-law's; maybe the weather wasn't right. Thankfully, we still had plenty of beans left in the original zipper bag. We could always try again next year.

At the same time humility leads us to embrace desire, it also teaches us how powerless we are to make our desires come to fruition. We can plan. We can build a trellis. We can plant beans. We can do all the right things. But we are not guaranteed a harvest simply because we worked hard and planned well. James puts it this way:

> Come now, you who say, "Today or tomorrow we will go into such and such a town and spend a year there and trade and make a profit" [and plant Mrs. Clovis Richards' beans]—yet you do not know what tomorrow will bring. What is your life? For you are a mist that appears for a little time and then vanishes. Instead you ought to say, "If the Lord wills, we will live and do this or that." As it is, you boast in your arrogance. All such boasting is evil.[6]

Pride tells us that all we have to do is organize well enough, plan effectively enough, and work hard enough and we can achieve our dreams. Humility teaches us that it was never up to us in the first place. The same God who gives us our desires is the God who orchestrates how, and whether, those desires come to pass. And the hard truth is that they may not.

You may never marry.

You may never achieve financial stability.

You may never have children.

You may never reach professional success.

You may never become a pastor in Virginia.

Part of the reason Nathan struggled to speak his desire in the first place was because it was risky. *What if it didn't happen? What if he failed? What if the pain of disappointment was more than he could bear?*

But here again, humility offers rest. If we are submitted to

---

6. James 4:13–16

God's hand, even our unfulfilled desires can be fruitful because our unfulfilled desires can be the very things God uses to draw us to Himself. When we've spent our lives and emotion and time and money pursuing what we believe will make us happy only to never reach it, we quickly learn where—better still, who—is the source of our ultimate joy. When we are denied the very things our hearts long for, we learn to long for the one thing that will never be denied us, God Himself. "It is good to be tired and wearied by the vain search after the true good," Blaise Pascal, the seventeenth-century philosopher-theologian assures us, "that we may stretch out our arms to the Redeemer." So when hope deferred makes our hearts sick, we learn to run to the Great Physician for healing.[7]

Hill of Beans

The same summer we first planted Mrs. Clovis Richards' beans, we leveled a 12 x 12 piece of ground outside our kitchen door to make a brick patio. After we had finished, we hauled away the excess dirt but the grass around the patio had become so trampled and covered with soil that we planned to reseed it in the fall. There was also a small mound of dirt that we'd saved back to eventually fill in divots in the yard, but that was work for another time.

Somehow in the middle of summer, the plastic zipper bag of Mrs. Richards' beans ended up on our patio table and, between three children and a beagle, had gotten a hole in it. Before either of us had discovered it, our then eight-year-old son found it and did what any eight-year-old boy should do: he proceeded to enlarge the hole and play with the beans that spilled out. Within a few days, we noticed tiny green sprouts in the dirt pile next to our

---

7. Proverbs 13:12.

new patio. They didn't look like weeds or grass, and sure enough, as they grew bigger and bigger, it became clear that they were bean sprouts. Apparently, our son had also been playing farmer.

It was all funny enough. At first. But then those beans—those cast off, forgotten, unattended beans—blossomed and produced more pods than my husband's carefully cultivated beans had. It was silly and laughable and humbling all at the same time. But when he saw how healthy they were, Nathan could do nothing but acquiesce to the whims of Providence and drive a stake in the middle of the dirt pile. Mrs. Clovis Richards' beans quickly climbed it, and we ate fresh green beans for the rest of the summer.

Part of humility means trusting God with our plans and submitting to the possibility that they will not be fulfilled. We pursue certain ends, but we can't know the future. But part of humility also means trusting God with our plans and submitting to the possibility that they will be fulfilled in ways we cannot imagine. Because we can't know the future, we also don't know when He will choose to bless us with abundance despite all signs pointing to failure. The writer of Ecclesiastes speaks to this possibility in the first four verses of chapter 11:

> Cast your bread upon the waters, for you will find it after many days. Give a portion to seven, or even to eight, for you know not what disaster may happen on earth. If the clouds are full of rain, they empty themselves on the earth, and if a tree falls to the south or to the north, in the place where the tree falls, there it will lie. He who observes the wind will not sow, and he who regards the clouds will not reap.

Humble people understand that their work is no guarantee of success; but the humble also understand that the possibility of failure is no reason not to work. Actuary tables notwithstanding, you simply cannot know what the future holds—good or bad. You simply cannot know. Only God knows His plans for tomorrow. So the writer of Ecclesiastes continues in verse 6, "in the morning sow your seed, and at evening withhold not your hand, for you do not know which will prosper, this or that, or whether both alike will be good."

You must "cast your bread upon the waters, for you will find it after many days." You must throw your beans in a pile of dirt and watch God grow them.

The fact that success comes without our efforts is testimony, yet again, to God's surpassing power and goodness. God delights to use small, out-of-the-way, unexpected means to showcase His glory precisely because it is small, out-of-the-way, unexpected means that appear to be least possible of success. And so He lets stay-at-home moms with degrees in humanities write books, and He lets men with a love for the country shepherd His flock there. He delights to do "far more abundantly than all that we ask or think"[8] simply to show that He can.

If we limit ourselves to working only when the signs are promising, if we only plant when everything is perfect, we limit our ability to see God at His best. When we limit ourselves to working when the time is right, we reveal that we are still clinging to the notion that success is dependent on our choices and our ability to control outcomes. We are still relying on our ability to make all the right decisions. We are still counting on our calculations and plans to foresee all possible eventualities.

But what if God can grow Mrs. Clovis Richards' beans in a pile of unattended dirt? What if God can bring about good things without us? What if grace is true?

---

8. Ephesians 3:20.

Time to Come

"She is not afraid of snow for her household . . . she
laughs at the time to come." —Proverbs 31:21, 25

Up in the mountains where Nathan grew up, where Mrs. Clovis
Richards' beans first took root, the older folks talk about "leather
britches" or long garlands of dried green beans. Before the days of
pressure cookers and sterilized glass jars and chest freezers, people preserved their produce by drying or salting it. To keep green
beans, they'd leave them whole and string them on heavy string
with a darning needle. Then they'd hang these pairs of "leather
britches" along the rafters or in the attic, tucked away safely for
the future. In the cold, dark days of winter, when you could barely
remember what a summer afternoon felt like, they'd take a handful
of them and stew them in a pot with a ham bone and maybe an
onion.

In many ways, the act of preserving food is an act of humility
and trust. We freeze and can and dry and pickle our green beans
because we believe that God has a future for us. Winter will come
and we will need them. At the same time, we know that our work
doesn't make the winter come. And it doesn't make spring come
again either. We know that even as we plan, an even Greater Plan-
ner is at work.

For my thoughts are not your thoughts, neither are your ways my
ways, declares the LORD. For as the heavens are higher than the
earth, so are my ways higher than your ways, and my thoughts
than your thoughts. For as the rain and the snow come down
from heaven and do not return there but water the earth, making
it bring forth and sprout, giving seed to the sower and bread to
the eater, so shall my word be that goes out from my mouth; it

shall not return to me empty, but it shall accomplish that which I purpose, and shall succeed in the thing for which I sent it.[9]

And so to grow and preserve green beans is also to experience grace. The grace to rest in the future that He has planned for us. The grace to work. The grace to wait. The grace to dream.

---

9. Isaiah 55:8–11.

FIGURE 10

Blackberries, *Rubus allegheniensis*

Chapter 10

Thorns and Thistles

"Nobody in the lane, and nothing, nothing but blackberries / Blackberries on either side, though on the right mainly."
—*Sylvia Plath*

A s the late July sun beat down, a trickle of sweat slid down my neck and along my backbone. Despite the heat, I was dressed in heavy pants and a long-sleeved cotton shirt; my hair was tucked up under both a scarf and hat. I heard a mosquito buzz and then fall suspiciously silent, more than likely feasting on a patch of skin that, despite my best efforts, was still exposed. I couldn't shoo her along or pull my shirt away from my increasingly damp back, though, because my left arm was holding the thicket while my right reached for a cluster of fruit swinging from the prickly cane in front of me. As I shifted my weight to reach it, my boots sank deeper into the soft pastureland, threatening to throw me off balance entirely. I righted myself and checked to see that the bucket at my feet was still upright as well. I could not risk spilling it. I'd already had to rescue it once from a curious cow who'd wandered too close; but curious cows are also clumsy cows, and the work I was doing required care and precision.

It was blackberry season.

That night, after I'd returned home with my bucket full, I showered and applied cream to my hands. I'd already removed several large thorns, but smaller ones remained embedded, the flesh around them increasingly red and swollen. The pads of my fingers were purply-black where berry juice had settled into the ridges, making it look as if I'd been fingerprinted, a thief who'd stolen nature's bounty. Despite my long sleeves, the backs of my hands and forearms were scratched in narrow trails of dried blood, and I remembered why women used to wear gloves to church and town. But as I looked at my stained hands and felt the sting of them, I also remembered my grandmother.

On summer mornings in late July, my grandmother (the same who made us stewed tomatoes) would get up early, dress in heavy pants and long sleeves, wrap her hair in a thin scarf, and don a wide-brimmed hat. Then she'd take her gallon buckets and go tramping along the edges of fields and fence rows in search of blackberries (*Rubus allegheniensis*). After several hours, she'd return, buckets full. She'd scrub her hands and feet with a diluted bleach solution to wash them clean of poison ivy, shower, grab a bite to eat, and if I was lucky, take me with her to sell her berries along the main road. We always went to the same place—a spot where the shoulder widened, creating a gravel pull-off—and she'd set up her card table and portion the berries out into white Styrofoam containers.

Grandma tasked me with holding the poster board sign she attached to a long wooden 2 x 2, carefully stenciled letters announcing:

BLACKBERRIES

QT $1.60

PT $.90

She showed me how to turn the sign toward oncoming traffic and then rotate it as travelers sped past to make sure they had full knowledge of what they were missing. Eventually, someone would stop, comment on how long it had been since they'd eaten blackberries, and drive away, savoring the bittersweet taste of memory. After several hours or when we sold out, Grandma would pack up the card table, slip it into her trunk, and take me down the road to Jenny Elaine's diner. If we hadn't sold enough, she'd pack up the card table, slip it into her trunk, and we'd go home to turn the leftover berries into pies, cobblers, and jam.

More than anything, though—more than the boredom of sitting along the road, more than the sweet-and-sour pleasure of a stolen blackberry, more than the satisfaction of a customer finally stopping—more than anything, I remember my grandma's hands. They were always clean, painfully so; but they were also scratched and scarred, pierced with a hundred tiny thorns.

Cursed Is the Ground

"By the pricking of my thumbs / Something wicked this way comes."
—*Second witch in Shakespeare's Macbeth*

Throughout Scripture, thorns illustrate the brokenness of the world, and with good reason. After the man and woman lifted themselves up against God, a kind of pestilence fell over the creation, a curse that included thorns and thistles. "Cursed is the ground because of you," God promises, and "in pain you shall eat of it all the days of your life; thorns and thistles it shall bring forth for you; and you shall eat the plants of the field."[1]

The problem, of course, is that the brokenness of the world

---

1. Genesis 3:17–18.

isn't simply a small irritation, a thorn that eventually works its way out of our skin. Open a news app on your phone, log onto social media, live in relationship with any other human being and you know the far-reaching and devastating effects of the fall. You know how men and women work for years to build their homes and communities, but then in a second, must grab their children and flee the ravages of war. Natural disasters, famine, and disease leave tens of thousands dead or wounded or homeless, sometimes with little warning. And on a smaller scale, one moment of passion, one choice to deceive, can break trust and send a ripple effect through a family for generations. Thorns? More like knives and swords.

Philosophers and theologians use the word "theodicy" to describe the brokenness of the world and the problem of evil. If God exists, if He truly is God, if He is good and kind and powerful, why is the world such a messed-up place? Certainly, we can point to human pride as a source of brokenness, but why let that pride flourish? Why not cut it off? If you could stop something bad from happening, why wouldn't you?

World religions all offer different answers to this question. In the Greco-Roman world, human suffering was largely seen as a product of fate, the whim of gods and goddesses whose interactions with humans were rooted in their own jealousies and infighting. Broadly speaking, Hinduism centers the weight of suffering on the individual's choice; through karma and the cycle of reincarnation, we experience the results of our previous actions, both good and bad. Buddhism is less concerned with explaining evil, focusing instead on breaking the cycle of suffering; we must simply accept brokenness as a normal part of human experience and transcend it.

In general, Christianity understands suffering as the interplay between a good Creator God, fallen mankind, and the supernatural forces of evil. But even within orthodox thought, there are still many different explanations for the problem of pain, none of them entirely sufficient. "Trying to solve the problem of evil," a theology professor I once knew would say, "is like trying to pick up three watermelons with two arms." You must hold to God's power; you must also hold that God is good, personally invested in His creation; but you must also hold the fact that evil exists. No matter how you try to juggle it, no human answer is entirely satisfying. And at some point, you're left wondering, "What's the use?" At some point, you're left wondering, "Why even try if you're only going to get scratched and scarred?"

Like so many other things, we can respond to the brokenness of the world either in pride and self-reliance or we can respond in humility. And how we choose to respond will have direct correlation to our sense of peace in the midst of it.

A Day's Labor

"The essential heresy [is] that work is not the expression of man's creative energy in service of society, but only something one does to obtain money and leisure." —Dorothy L. Sayers

My mom and aunt always fussed that my grandma didn't price her blackberries high enough. And they were absolutely right. Grandma would spend hours in the blazing sun, suffer the pricks of briers, regularly contract poison ivy, and patiently wait beside the road, only to sell an entire quart of succulent blackberries for one dollar and sixty cents. These were no hot-house blackberries, my aunt and mom would remind her. These were not tasteless, domesticated pretenders. These were wild blackberries. Folks would pay a premium for them, they told her, if she only asked.

But for whatever reason, Grandma wouldn't. She didn't seem

to mind that she was, to my mom's and aunt's minds, getting taken. I don't know if it was because my grandma lacked confidence or she undervalued her own work or she worried that folks would balk at a higher price. It might have been that she thought of the berries as coming to her "free" and so she didn't think she had a right to charge more. All she'd done was pick them, after all.

I tend to think that she priced her berries low as an act of good will, a gesture of kindness to all the folks who were too busy with their hectic lives to pick blackberries for themselves. Maybe, in her own way, she wanted to bring them a bit of happiness, to remind them of times past, of their own mothers and grandmothers. Maybe she did it for the sheer love of blackberries. Grandma simply didn't feel the need to profit from her blackberries. Every summer she'd faithfully pick them. Every summer, she'd set up her table beside the road. Every summer, she'd sell them for $1.60 a quart and $ .90 per pint.

My grandma's refusal to increase the price of her blackberries runs opposite what most of us would do. After all, in a broken world, you've got to get what you can get. You shouldn't take advantage of the other guy, but you've got to take care of yourself. In fact, the temptation to pursue wealth as a means of combating brokenness is so common that Jesus alludes to it in one of His best-known parables. In Luke 8, Jesus tells the story of a sower who spreads seed on different types of ground. Some falls on good ground, but some, the text says, falls "among thorns, and the thorns grew up with it and choked it." Jesus explains that the seed is the word of God and the soil represents the state of the human heart.[2]

Referencing the thorny ground, Jesus says, "And as for what fell

---

2. Jesus uses dirt to describe the state of the human heart, alluding to creation and the fact that we were made from dust.

among the thorns, they are those who hear, but as they go on their way they are choked by the cares and riches and pleasures of life, and their fruit does not mature."[3]

Initially, Jesus' words don't make sense to us. We understand why Jesus uses thorns to describe the cares of life, but why link the cares of life with riches and pleasure? The answer lies in why we seek money and pleasure in the first place. For many people, pleasure and wealth is a way to deal with life in a hostile world. If the world is dangerous and God is not present—either from impotency or disinterest—then we are left to cope on our own, to grasp all the happiness we can. In other words, "If I have to depend on myself to make it through this world, then I'm going to get while the getting's good. I'm going to live it up." And in our pride, we overestimate our ability to find happiness and end up embracing a form of hedonism, believing that pleasure can inoculate us to the pain around us.

The danger of hedonism is so prevalent in fact, that Jesus again warns against it in Luke 21, cautioning His hearers that pursuing pleasure could actually end up having the opposite effect to what we want. Instead of keeping us safe from the danger of this world, the pursuit of pleasure could expose us to even greater danger by dulling our senses. "But watch yourselves," He tells them in verse 34, foretelling the coming destruction of Jerusalem, "lest your hearts be weighed down with dissipation and drunkenness and cares of this life, and that day come upon you suddenly like a trap." Watch yourselves. Watch out that in attempting to escape the cares of life you don't walk right into them.

It'd be easy to associate hedonism with the playboy and party girl lifestyle of Hollywood celebrity—the swagger, the lust, the

---

3. The parallel account in Matthew 13 describes the thorns as "the cares of the world and the deceitfulness of riches."

indulgence—but for most of us, hedonism cloaks itself in more respectable garb. Most of us are more likely to get trapped by consumerism, the daily visits to the stalls of Vanity Fair, than the nights of excess at the Playboy Mansion. We are more likely to get trapped by one more purse. One more tech gadget. One more trip. One more novel. One more piece of cake.

But these vanities cannot deliver the happiness they promise. And in our pursuit of them, we are the ones who end up caught— caught in cycles of debt, spending, and indulgence and all the stress that comes with it. We are the ones caught in the weight of ownership. Part of the way riches deceive us is that we end up caught caring for the very things that we thought would care for us. We find ourselves with drawers and closets full of clothing, cupboards and refrigerators full of food, and garages full of un-used sports gear and yard tools. And we feel the weight of it. We do not feel the weight of good gifts, for good gifts point back to the Giver; no, we feel the weight of trying to replace the Giver with His gifts. We feel the weight of the pride that convinced us to rely on earthly goods to relieve a spiritual need in the first place. And we find ourselves in a constant cycle of maintaining these earthly goods, of packing and moving them and sending them off to Goodwill so we can have space to buy more. We find ourselves caught work, work, working to afford them, our hands "full of toil and a striving after the wind."[4]

Whatever.

"Only the humble believe . . . that God is so free and so marvelous that he does wonders where people despair, that he takes what is little and lowly and makes it marvelous." —Dietrich Bonhoeffer

---

4. Ecclesiastes 4:6.

And yet, as quickly as we find ourselves working to consume, we can just as quickly find ourselves lazy; we can just as easily give up hope that there is any happiness worth finding. Remember that pride both overestimates our abilities and underestimates God. If hedonism convinces us that we can achieve happiness on our own, sloth deceives us about God's ability to make our efforts effective in a broken world. Rooted in pride, sloth factors God out of the equation entirely. If God is not present or powerful here, there is no guarantee that your work or time will be rewarded. So why even try? Why even work?

King Solomon notes the connection between laziness and brokenness in Proverbs 24:30–31:

> I passed by the field of a sluggard,
> > by the vineyard of a man lacking sense,
> and behold it was all overgrown with thorns;
> > the ground was covered with nettles,
> > and its stone wall was broken down.

We often see laziness as a lack of initiative or even a lack of confidence. But it's actually the reverse. The sluggard thinks so highly of his energy and efforts that he's not willing to waste them. He's not willing to expend energy unless he has a guaranteed reward. Because, in his pride, he has foolishly discounted God, he no longer has reason to believe that his work will amount to anything. So he simply cuts his losses trusting that "a little sleep, a little slumber" (24:33) will bring him rest. But not working doesn't lead to rest. It leads to poverty and want. It leads to messy houses and broken-down churches and chaotic lives. And left unchecked it can blossom into the full-formed despair early Christian monks called "acedia."

Perhaps the final and fullest expression of human pride is

complete and utter hopelessness, a view of the world that has so dismissed God that nothing matters anymore. Because pride leads us to reject God, we end up trusting ourselves. But it is only a matter of time before we realize how misplaced this trust is. And when we do, when the brokenness of the world presses in, when we feel the weight of our own helplessness, we succumb to listlessness and despondency. Nothing has purpose. Nothing has meaning. Nothing is worth doing. Why sweep the floor? It will just get dirty again. Why prepare a Sunday school lesson? The children don't pay attention anyway. Why pray? God probably won't even hear me.

In an interview with the *Los Angeles Times*, Kathleen Norris, author of *Acedia & Me: A Marriage, Monks, and a Writer's Life*, speaks of acedia this way:

> When you tell people you're writing about the spiritual aspect of sloth, they don't know what you mean. But when you say "indifference," they do. They understand not being able to care, and being so not able to care that you don't care that you don't care.[5]

This indifference may come after years of public ministry. It may come after weeks of new parenthood. It may come in the middle of an extended illness. It may come when you finally realize that your hopes of marriage will never be fulfilled. But when it comes, when this acedia descends, it will stalk you like "the pestilence that stalks in darkness . . . the destruction that wastes at noonday."[6] More subtle and beguiling than direct temptation, acedia creeps in and dulls the soul, making it almost impossible to care about anything.

---

5. Lynell George, "Kathleen Norris battles 'the demon of acedia'," *Los Angeles Times*, September 21, 2008.
6. Acedia has long been known as the "noonday demon" in reference to Psalm 91:6.

shrug
sigh
Whatever.

Norris also notes that the word "acedia" went all but obsolete by the 1930s but resurged again after World War II.

> The violence had been so horrible all over the world. The Holocaust in Europe and the atomic bomb in Japan. And in America . . . we were supposed to forget about all of our troubles by buying a dishwasher.

The disconnect is simply too much. Without a strong understanding of God's presence in our brokenness, without the humility to recognize His power, nothing matters. And mundane things like dishwashers and monthly reports and PTA meetings feel especially meaningless. *But what if God is present in the brokenness? And what if He isn't simply present but He's actively defeating it? What if humility teaches us to believe that God can bring fruit from briers?*

Crown of Thorns

"Humility is something infinitely deeper than contrition . . . it [is] participation in the life of Jesus." —Andrew Murray

While no human answer to the problem of evil is entirely satisfying, this doesn't mean that there are no answers. We may not understand it all, but we cling to what we do know. And what we do know—what Christians throughout history have clung to—is that the God of the universe does not abandon us in our suffering. We may not know why suffering happens; we may not know how to free ourselves from it; but we do know that Jesus entered our brokenness and took it on Himself. We do know that "He humbled himself by becoming obedient to the point of death, even death on a cross."

There may be no better illustration of Jesus suffering under the weight of the curse than what we read in Matthew's account of Jesus' trial:

> Pilate said to them, "Then what shall I do with Jesus who is
> called Christ?" They all said, "Let him be crucified!" And he said,
> "Why, what evil has he done?" But they shouted all the more,
> "Let him be crucified!" . . . Then the soldiers of the governor
> took Jesus into the governor's headquarters . . . and they stripped
> him and put a scarlet robe on him, and twisting together a crown
> of thorns, they put it on his head.[7]

A crown of thorns. Do not underestimate the significance of this crown of thorns. This was not simply a way to inflict pain, to press barbs into His profoundly human flesh. This was an attempt to humiliate Him and mock His power. What better way to diminish the King of the universe than to crown Him with the very curse that hangs over His creation? What better way to triumph over Him than for evil to adorn His head? What could be more humiliating than to have our brokenness rest on Him?

But it is from these very thorns that Jesus proves His power. It is from these very thorns that He shows how humility overcomes the brokenness. It is from these very thorns that He produces sweet, abundant fruit. And so, in His humility, He opens not His mouth. "When he was reviled," Peter writes, "he did not revile in return; when he suffered, he did not threaten, but continued

---

7. Matthew 27:22–23; 27–29.

entrusting himself to him who judges justly."[8]

This is how humility overcomes the world: Humility trusts God.

In the midst of injustice, humility believes that God is just. In the midst of grief, humility believes that God is comfort. In the midst of brokenness, humility believes that God is health and life. "The ultimate cause of spiritual depression," Dr. D. Martyn Lloyd-Jones writes in his classic *Spiritual Depression*, "is unbelief . . ." And so you must

> take yourself in hand, you have to address yourself, preach to yourself, question yourself. . . . And then you must go on to remind yourself of God, Who God is and what God is and what God has done, and what God has pledged Himself to do.[9]

And when we remember who God is, when we are humbled before Him, we will be free to mourn the brokenness—both from within and without.

Confessing Our Faults

"Confess your faults one to another, and pray one for another, that ye may be healed." —James 5:16 (KJV)

As a pastor's wife, I'm regularly surprised by how people behave around me. For some reason, they often feel the need to project a certain image or to protect me from their brokenness. When they do share the messier parts of their lives, they're often uncomfortable, almost embarrassed. At first, I took this personally, but then I realized

---

8. 1 Peter 2:23.
9. David Martyn Lloyd-Jones, *Spiritual Depression: Its Causes and Cure* (Grand Rapids, MI: Eerdmans, 1965), 20–21.

that it is more likely the product of their relationship to the church at large. For many people, the church is a place where they must keep their act together. They must put on a joyful face even when they are overwhelmed. They must have faith even when they doubt. They cannot risk being broken.

One of the main reasons we struggle to create safe communities is because we've underestimated God's power in brokenness and end up trusting in ourselves. But when we do, we can never admit failure. We can never admit need. We can never be weak. But it is precisely our brokenness that humbles us, and it is precisely our brokenness that reveals God's power. Paul writes about how the power of Christ rests upon him because of—not in spite of—his weakness:

> To keep me from becoming conceited because of the surpassing greatness of the revelations, a thorn was given me in the flesh, a messenger of Satan to harass me. . . . Three times I pleaded with the Lord about this, that it should leave me. But he said to me, "My grace is sufficient for you, for my power is made perfect in weakness."[10]

Humility teaches us that God is actively redeeming the world. And because He is, we can experience the relief of confessing our brokenness—whether it is intentional sin, our natural limitations, or simply the weight of living under the curse. Humility teaches us to find rest in confession. Rest from the need to hide, the need to be perfect. We rest by saying, both to God and others, "I am not enough. I need help."

And ultimately, the humility that leads us to confess our brokenness, both within and without, also frees us to grieve it and

---

10. 2 Corinthians 12:7–9.

throw ourselves on the mercy of God. And this, more than anything, leads to rest. When humility expresses itself in godly sorrow, we can finally break down; we can finally let it all out; we can finally have that "good" cry. Good, both because it is a weeping, breath-sucking catharsis, but also because it is legitimate. Good, because it honestly faces the brokenness of the world while resting in something—Someone—greater. Good, because it leads to surrender.

To cry like Jesus as He looks over Jerusalem. To cry like Jesus as He stands at Lazarus's tomb. To cry like Jesus as He endures the cross and entrusts Himself to the Father.

And yet, even as we mourn the brokenness both within and without, we do not mourn without hope. The prophet Isaiah speaks of a day when "the light of Israel will become a fire and his Holy One a flame, and it will burn and devour his thorns and briers."[11] And when He does, we will

> go out in joy and be led forth in peace;
> the mountains and the hills before you
>   shall break forth into singing,
>   and all the trees of the field shall clap
>   their hands.
> Instead of the thorn shall come up the
>   cypress;
>   instead the brier shall come up the
>   myrtle;
>   and it shall make a name for the LORD,
>   an everlasting sign that shall not be
>   cut off.[12]

---

11. Isaiah 10:17.
12. Isaiah 55:12–13.

Foraging Grace

"I love to go out in late September / among the fat, overripe, icy, black blackberries / to eat blackberries for breakfast." —Galway Kinnell

Of course, over the years, growers have developed thornless blackberries. You can buy them and grow them in your side yard, eliminating the need for heavy pants and long sleeves entirely. But I've always thought that this is cheating somehow. Blackberries are meant to be foraged, to grow in dense thickets on the edges of civilization, along fields, in scrub patches, beside abandoned barns and forgotten hay rakes. The thick, heavy thorns on the canes are meant to catch your legs, the smaller ones to pierce your hands as you grasp their alluring fruit. Suffering and delight bound up in the same plant.

Historians tell us that part of the way the Pilgrims survived their first summer was by eating blackberries, and my grandfather on my mother's side told us that he survived the Great Depression by eating blackberry cobbler. A bit of flour, a pat of lard, salt, milk, and the abundance of the forest. Blackberries with their prickly canes and lush fruit embody God's grace in the midst of our suffering. Even in the brokenness, there is life. Even in the brokenness, there is goodness. Even in the brokenness, there is hope.

The humble person doesn't deny the pain of this world, or her complicity in it, but she does hope. She continues to forage for the sweetness that God has promised. She gleans where she has not planted. Along the fence rows and roadsides. Not in carefully cultivated thickets, but in the wildness of the waysides. Our hands may be scratched and bleeding, we may stink of sweat, our feet sinking in the mud, but there, just within our grasp, is a cluster of hope—a reminder of who God is and how He never fails His children.

FIGURE 11

Crocus, *Crocus vernus*

Chapter 11

A Secret Garden

"The wailing grew wilder and wilder. . . . Someone has died." —Frances H. Burnett

I was eleven, just days shy of turning twelve, when I skipped up the crooked cement sidewalk that ringed the back of my grandma's white, clapboard bungalow. In my memory, her house had always been white with a green front porch and green trim around the windows, but I'd seen a picture once—from when my dad was young—when it had been covered in insulbrick siding with nothing more than a stoop in the front yard. This particular day was a soggy afternoon in early March; the ground was soaked from piles of melting snow, and the air cool but no longer the cold of winter. Beside the walkway, a handful of crocuses had already pushed their purple heads through the dampness, signaling that spring was near.

My dad had started up the walk before me, but by the time I'd reached the kitchen door (we never entered by the front door) he was still standing at it, knocking. When there was no answer, he simply removed his key from his pocket and let himself in. By this time, my older brother had tagged along, too, and we followed our dad into the kitchen. Several baskets of neatly folded laundry sat on the table; there were no dirty dishes in sight. Just as you'd expect in Grandma's kitchen. My brother and I wandered into the living room, just off the kitchen, and I plopped myself on the end of her brocade couch.

These are the moments I remember. The moments before my dad entered the living room and told my brother to call emergency services. The moments before he reappeared and grabbed the phone from his hand and spoke into the receiver: "I think my mother has passed." These are the moments just before he'd found my grandmother still and lifeless in her bed. As my dad's words registered in my consciousness, something broke inside me. Sounds came from me that, until then, I did not know my vocal chords could utter. Of course I'd cried before—tears of anger, injustice, and embarrassment even—but compared to what issued from my throat that day, they were nothing. It was as though I was listening to someone else. My shoulders shook, my stomach plummeted. Something was profoundly and cosmically wrong. My grandma—she of blackberries and stewed tomatoes—could not be gone.

I wish I could say that the days that followed were a blur, but they were not. I remember them in painstaking detail; my senses were sharp, almost as if they were on high alert. A world that had once been safe, no longer was. I remember my dad driving us home. The greasy smell of my mother cooking an egg for my little sister. Extended family coming to be with us. The friends and relatives crowding into Blair-Lowther funeral home. The bizarre ritual of them silently filing in front of my grandma's body. Of course, there was plenty of activity. It wasn't as if these days happened in slow motion, despite my heightened senses. The adults had plenty to do—make arrangements and order flowers and cook food—the work that kept their grief at bay at least for a while. But as a child, there was little I could do. Nothing. Nothing to do but endure.

Sitting in the funeral home, on one of a hundred identically upholstered chairs, I looked at the flowers that surrounded her casket. They were beautiful in their own way, I supposed, but they seemed so unlike her. This woman spent her days outside, not indoors. This woman had gardened and foraged and grown up on the mountain. This woman's hands were rough and worn from a lifetime of good work. Greenhouse flowers seemed too civilized somehow, domesticated and tame. And I knew what I wanted to do; I wanted to gather flowers for her.

If it had been a few months later, I'd have collected wild daisies, ironweed, yarrow, and Queen Anne's lace. But it was early March, and the fields and woods had not yet blossomed. Except in one place. I remembered the crocuses I passed beside the crooked side-walk. Just days before, they'd popped their heads up to alert us that spring was coming; but not before winter had struck one final blow and had stolen my blackberry grandmother away.

When we returned home between viewings, I picked the cro-cuses. There weren't many, but there were enough. A few solid purple ones; one variegated white and purple; all with bright yellowy-orange centers. I wrapped a ribbon around them as best I could, careful not to crush the fragile stems, and put them in the refrigerator to keep their delicate petals from wilting. When we returned later to the funeral home, my aunt—the same who would one day advise me to marry a doctor—walked me to the casket. Standing before my grandma, I could almost believe that I could see her chest rising and falling. Maybe it was all a mistake. Maybe . . . but it wasn't. And there was nothing left to do for her except place my offering of crocuses in her stiff hands. There was nothing left to do. Nothing, except this small gesture of hope that one day spring would come again for her.

Into the Earth

"In the spring, at the end of the day, you should smell like dirt."
—*Margaret Atwood*

Of all human experiences, death is the most humbling. To be so finally and completely stripped of our ability, to be so tangibly reminded that we are nothing "but dust." No other experience can do for us what death does. I wonder sometimes if this is why we must die. Why the punishment for our pride is final and total humility. Why the cure for our pride is final and total humility. But it doesn't happen all at once. Death humbles us by bits. It humbles us over the course of a lifetime as friends and loved ones slip away and we remember that we will one day too. This is part of what Solomon means when he writes that

> It is better to go to the house of mourning
>> than to go to the house of feasting,
> for this is the end of all mankind,
>> and the living will lay it to heart.[1]

Standing beside my grandma's casket, I faced not only her mortality, but my own as well. *Is this why we keep so busy around a death—why we make arrangements and cook and visit and pace? Do we simply need to remember our own aliveness?* To stop long enough to mourn is too difficult. To surrender to grief, even momentarily, reminds us that one day we must surrender finally and fully. But even as we resist it, death does its work. Even as we resist, death humbles us. As we watch our friends weaken, we remember our own weakness. As we watch loved ones snatched away, we rec-

---

1. Ecclesiastes 7:2.

ognize our lack of control. As we watch strong, beautiful people humbled in a moment, we know that we will be humbled one day as well.

And one day death's final blow—the one we each must take for ourselves—will remove from us the final vestiges of pride.

And so I wonder, too, if this is why Jesus *had* to die. Why the redemption of a proud people could only come by a great humbling. Why the grip of pride could only be broken by an act of greater humility. This must also be why the apostle Paul connects Jesus' humility with His death: "And being found in human form, he humbled himself by becoming obedient to the point of death, even death on the cross." Or as Luke tells it in his gospel: "Then Jesus, calling out with a loud voice, said, 'Father, into your hands I commit my spirit!' And having said this he breathed his last."[2]

Father, into your hands I commit my spirit.

All our life, humility is working to this end: Father, into Your hands I commit my spirit.

I give up.

I surrender.

I trust.

At the end of my grandma's funeral, after we sang "The Old Rugged Cross" and cried and strangers had closed her casket, we filed out of the funeral home to waiting cars. We drove a few miles up the road and put her body into the earth. Or in the words of the *Book of Common Prayer*, we "commit[ted] her body to the ground; earth to earth, ashes to ashes, dust to dust." And it's this moment, I think, that the reality of death finally hits. When you put the body—the body that dreamed and worked and ate and sang and loved—when you put that body into the ground and walk away from it. We scarcely can think about it, scarcely think about what

---

2. Luke 23:46.

happens after we walk away. The rotting and decaying and returning to dust. Even if we choose cremation, the end is the same: ashes
to ashes and dust to dust and so let's just get it over with.

And so I wonder, too, if this is why Jesus *had* to be buried—
why we must see Him enter the earth. Luke continues his narrative: "Now there was a man named Joseph, from the Jewish town
of Arimathea. . . . This man went to Pilate and asked for the body
of Jesus. Then he took it down and wrapped it in a linen shroud
and laid him in a tomb."[3] And here we see the liturgy of humility.
Here we see the acting out of humility. He *descended* to earth to
lead captives free. He was taken *down*. He was *laid* in a tomb.
And so too, we, who are dust, return to the dust. We, who raised
ourselves up, are lowered into the ground. At death, we go down,
deep, to "smell like dirt" once again.

And we finally become what we truly are.

But when this happens, when the creature is finally and fully
humbled, the world rights itself. When Jesus humbled Himself
and submitted to death, He unleashed a power greater than death.
For this has been God's longstanding promise: "Humble yourselves, therefore, under the mighty hand of God so that at the
proper time he may exalt you."[4] This has been God's longstanding
promise: "Whoever exalts himself will be humbled, and whoever
humbles himself will be exalted."[5] And so

> Death, be not proud, though some have called thee
> Mighty and dreadful, for thou art not so;
> For those whom thou think'st thou dost overthrow
> Die not, poor Death, nor yet canst thou kill me . . .[6]

---

3. Luke 23:50, 52–53.
4. 1 Peter 5:6.
5. Matthew 23:12.
6. John Donne, Holy Sonnet 10, "Death Be Not Proud."

Even as we are humbled in death, God promises that death—that proud destroyer—will itself one day be humbled. Even as death boasts over us, God promises that one day death will be abased and we, who have been humbled, will be exalted.

"It is a strange thing to cut out the blocks of sod and then dig my way to the dark layer where the dead lie," reflects Jayber Crow, the gravedigger of Wendell Berry's fictional Port William, Kentucky. "I feel a little uneasy in calling them 'the dead,' for I am as mystified as anybody by the transformation known as death, and the Resurrection is more real to me than most things I have not yet seen."[7]

As real as springtime.

Crocus vernus

> *"I smell something nice and fresh and damp," she said.*
> *"That's th' good rich earth," he answered, digging away.*
> *"You'll see bits o' green spikes stickin' out o' th' black earth*
> *after a bit . . . crocuses an' snowdrops an' daffydowndillys."*
> —*Frances H. Burnett, The Secret Garden*

Though the crocuses (*Crocus vernus*) that grew beside my grandma's white clapboard house are not native to these mountains, they are ubiquitous. First cultivated in the Mediterranean, these small, cup-shaped flowers are a favorite, in part, because they are hardy, easy to grow, and self-propagating. Put a few bulbs into the ground, and you'll soon have a garden. Crocuses are among the first flowers to poke their heads through the ground at winter's end. Undaunted by the lingering cold, their enthusiasm is infectious,

---

7. Wendell Berry, *Jayber Crow: A Novel* (Washington, DC: Counterpoint, 2000), 157.

and it's not unusual to see their vivid petals encased in ice and snow.

The resilience of crocuses plays an important role in Frances Hodgson Burnett's classic *The Secret Garden*.[8] When petulant ten-year-old Mary Lennox is orphaned, she comes to live with her widowed uncle at Misselthwaite Manor, the ancestral home on the Yorkshire moors. The house and grounds are as full of mystery as is her uncle Archibald. Because he is gone so often, the house staff cares for Mary and she is given free rein of the estate's gardens. Except for one. There is one garden that is walled off from the rest of the estate that has been shut and locked for ten years. But through Providence and the help of a fat, cheery robin, the garden doesn't stay locked long. Mary discovers the key in a plot of freshly turned earth, and the door, soon after. But when she enters, the garden looks as if it is dead. The walls are covered in gray vines; weeds have encroached on the flower beds, and the trees are brittle and leafless. But then Mary notices tiny shoots of green.

> She thought she saw something sticking out of the black earth— some sharp little pale green points. She remembered what Ben Weatherstaff [the gardener] had said and she knelt down to look at them. "Yes, they are tiny growing things and they might be crocuses or snowdrops or daffodils," she whispered.

Later Mary asks her maid, Martha, about the bulbs,

> "Do bulbs live a long time? Would they live years and years if no one helped them?" inquired Mary anxiously.
> "They're things as helps themselves," said Martha. "That's

---

8. Frances Hodges Burnett's *The Secret Garden* has delighted audiences since its first publication in 1911.

why poor folk can afford to have 'em. If you don't trouble 'em, most of 'em'll work away underground for a lifetime an' spread out an' have little 'uns. There's a place in th' park woods here where there's snowdrops by thousands. They're the prettiest sight . . . when th' spring comes. No one know when they was first planted."

Today, if you walk through the hills where I live, you'll stumble across beds of crocuses and daffodils just like Martha described. You'll see them beside the road, along fence posts, and clustered near solitary chimneys where settlers' homes once stood. There's no way to know how they got there, no way to know who first planted and tended these humble flowers—a small taste of civilization in the wild—but there they stand, keeping watch. There they grow. And every spring, there they are resurrected to brave the chilly wind.

And just as God raises the crocus every spring, without the assistance of gardener or tenant, God the Father raised Jesus from the dead. God would not abandon His soul to Hades or let His Holy One see corruption. "This Jesus," Peter proclaims to the breathless crowd, "This Jesus God raised up, and of that we all are witnesses!"[9]

But resurrection does not happen apart from humility. Resurrection does not happen apart from surrendering to the Father's will. In this sense, God the Father did not raise Jesus up simply because He was His Son; God raised Jesus up because this is how God responds to humility. He exalts those who humble themselves. This is the governing dynamic in God's upside-down kingdom: You go down in order to go up. You go low in order to go

---

9. Acts 2:27, 32.

high. You humble yourself in order to be exalted. Jesus explained it this way:

> When you are invited by someone to a wedding feast, do not sit down in a place of honor, lest someone more distinguished than you be invited by him. . . . But when you are invited, go and sit in the lowest place, so that when your host comes he may say to you, "Friend, move up higher." . . . For everyone who exalts himself will be humbled, and he who humbles himself will be exalted.[10]

And so because Jesus lowered Himself to the earth, because He went down as a seed to die,[11] "God has highly exalted him and bestowed on him the name that is above every name, so that at the name of Jesus every knee should bow, in heaven and on earth and under the earth, and every tongue confess that Jesus Christ is Lord, to the glory of God the Father."[12]

The Gardener

"The wilderness and the dry land shall be glad; the desert shall rejoice and blossom like the crocus; it shall blossom abundantly." —Isaiah 35:1–2

In his gospel, the apostle John recounts what happened immediately after God raised Jesus from the dead on that early morning in Jerusalem. A few of the women who followed Jesus come to anoint His body with spices but find the tomb empty. Mary Magdalene can stand it no longer—the weight of the trial, Jesus' hor-

---

10. Luke 14:8, 10–11.
11. John 12:24.
12. Philippians 2:9–11.

rific death, His burial—all of it is too much. And now she believes thieves have stolen away His body. She succumbs to weeping. Distraught she turns from the tomb and sees a man standing in front of her. Although she does not recognize him, it is Jesus.

"Woman, why are you weeping? Whom are you seeking?" Supposing him to be the gardener, she said to him, "Sir, if you have carried him away, tell me where you have laid him, and I will take him away." Jesus said to her, "Mary." She turned and said to him, "Rabboni!"[13]

"Supposing Him to be the gardener . . ."
As the story of *The Secret Garden* unfolds, little Mary enlists the help of Martha's younger brother, the animal charmer and green man, Dickon. "Our Dickon"—as Martha calls him—looks like any other twelve-year-old Yorkshire boy, but he has an unusual gift for cultivating life. "He can make a flower grow out of a brick walk," Martha assures Mary. "Mother says he just whispers things out o' th' ground." And under Dickon's skillful hand, we watch as both Mary and the secret garden come back to life.

Award-winning children's author Mitali Perkins notes the similarities between Dickon's and Jesus' own ability to cultivate life where death once reigned. "In *The Secret Garden*, Frances Hodgson Burnett perhaps subconsciously provided a metaphorical glimpse of the Trinity—Father (Susan Sowerby), Son (Dickon), and Holy Spirit (the robin)," Perkins says in an interview with *Christianity Today* in which she relates how she came to Christ from a Hindu background. "For years, these spiritual mothers and fathers had been teaching me about the Bible. I just didn't realize it."[14]

---

13. John 20:15–16.
14. Mitali Perkins, "When God Writes Your Life Story," *Christianity Today*, January/February 2016, 96.

"Supposing Him to be the gardener . . ."

Jesus' work to restore humility did not end with His own resurrection. Even today, even now, His work of resurrection continues. Even now, He is cultivating His garden. Even now, the second Adam, the true Son of Man, is tending His Eden. And as we submit to His skillful hand, our own hearts and lives—though perhaps for a time locked and dead—will break forth in green.

But this work involves death and resurrection. Like Dickon, Jesus is "very strong and clever with his knife and [knows] how to cut the dry and dead wood away." But we can trust Him. We can trust His process because it is through the process of dying and resurrection that we find rest. "Clothe yourselves, all of you," Peter appeals to us, "with humility toward one another, for 'God opposes the proud but gives grace to the humble.' Humble yourselves, therefore, under the mighty hand of God so that at the proper time he may exalt you, casting all your anxieties on him, because he cares for you."[15]

When we go down, God raises us up. When we submit to Him, He exalts us. Andrew Murray calls this phenomenon, this way of living, a "death-life"—a process by which we descend each day into that perfect, helpless dependence upon God, even as we trust Him to raise us from the earth itself.

"I think," says Mary, "the ground is full of daffodils and snow-drops and lilies and iris working their way out of the dark . . . perhaps there are clusters of purple crocuses and gold ones—even now. Perhaps the leaves are beginning to break out and uncurl— and perhaps—the gray is changing and a green gauze veil is creeping—and creeping over—everything.

---

15. 1 Peter 5:5–7.

Yes, Mary, yes, it is. The ground is full of bulbs working their way out of the dark. The green is creeping over everything. And one day, Jesus' work of tending His garden will be full and complete. One day, His promise through the prophet Isaiah will be fulfilled:

> Your dead shall live; their bodies shall rise.
>   You who dwell in dust, awake and sing for joy!
> For your dew is a dew of light,
>   and the earth will give birth to the dead.[16]

Near the end of *The Secret Garden*, Mary, Dickon, the under-gardener Ben Weatherstaff, and Mary's cousin Colin stand in the midst of a fragrant, flourishing garden. Just like the garden, Colin has been for years locked away in his rooms, hidden from sight, suffering under the weight of fear, anger, depression, and uncertainty. Through Dickon's and Mary's friendship and the "magic" of the garden, Colin regains both his health and his humanity. Standing there in the middle of the secret garden, he exclaims:

> "I shall live forever and ever and ever! I'm well! I'm well! I'm well! I feel—I feel as if I want to shout out something—something thankful, joyful!"
>
> Ben Weatherstaff, who had been working near a rose-bush, glanced round at him. "Tha' might sing th' Doxology," he suggested in his dryest grunt. He had no opinion of the Doxology and he did not make the suggestion with any particular reverence.
>
> But Colin was of an exploring mind and he knew nothing about the Doxology. "What is that?" he inquired.

---

16. Isaiah 26:19.

"Dickon can sing it for thee, I'll warrant," replied Ben Weatherstaff. Dickon answered with his all-perceiving animal charmer's smile.

"They sing it i' church," he said. "Mother says she believes th' skylarks sings it when they gets up i' th' mornin'."

Dickon stood out among the trees and rosebushes and began to sing in quite a simple matter-of-fact way and in a nice strong boy voice:

Praise God from whom all blessings flow,
Praise Him all creatures here below,
Praise Him above ye Heavenly Host,
Praise Father, Son, and Holy Ghost.
Amen.

At Rest

"Each morning sees some task begin / Each evening sees it close / Something attempted, something done / Has earned a night's repose." —Henry Wadsworth Longfellow

The irony is not lost on me that, twenty-five years after we found my grandmother forever at rest in her bed, I struggled to find rest in mine. For me, at least, the struggle to sleep was nothing more than a struggle to trust. To trust that I could lay myself down and close my eyes and the world would still be safe. To trust that I wasn't necessary to my own success. To trust that God was God and I wasn't.

Even as my body tossed and turned, the truth was that my soul was tossing and turning as well.

In many ways, the act of sleep is itself a spiritual act, an act of humility. To sleep, we must stop our work. To sleep, we must lay our bodies down. To sleep, we must trust another to care for us. And so we pray:

> Now I lay me down sleep,
> I pray the Lord my soul to keep.
> And if I die before I wake,
> I pray the Lord my soul to take.

And in God's wisdom, we must pray this every night. Every night, we must stop our work; every night, we must lay ourselves down; and every night, we must trust. Every night, we must practice. So that through our practicing He will make us perfect. Through practicing this trust every night, He is teaching us how to trust Him when He finally calls us to Himself. Through our practicing this rest every night, He is teaching us how to rest in Him for all eternity.

"So then, there remains a Sabbath rest for the people of God," the writer of Hebrews promises us, "for whoever has entered God's rest has also rested from his works as God did from his."[17] But this rest only comes by humility. This rest only comes by acknowledging our weakness. This rest only comes by submitting ourselves to Him.

For when you do, when you finally come to Him—you who labor and are heavy laden—you can be confident that He will welcome you. You can be confident that "the God of all grace, who has called you to his eternal glory in Christ, will himself restore, confirm, strengthen, and establish you."[18] You can be confident that His promise is true: When you come to Him, you will find rest for your soul.

---

17. Hebrews 4:9–10.
18. 1 Peter 5:10.

Acknowledgments

"Certain authors," writes French philosopher Blaise Pascal, "say, 'My book,' . . . They would do better to say, 'Our book' because there is in them usually more of other people's than their own." *Humble Roots* exists because of many people, most of whom would never identify as writers. But because of their contributions, you hold this book—*our* book—in your hands.

Nathan, any and all good work we do grows from the soil of our shared lives—picking stones, pulling weeds, and planting seeds.

Phoebe, Harry, and Peter, may you grow strong and flourish.

Friends near and far—

Heather, for getting me where I need to be (and when) and for loving my children,

Mandi, for listening so well,

Virginia, for your constant enthusiasm for my writing,

Melinda, for relishing and sharing memories of country life,

Kim, for quiet, faithful presence,

Erik W., agent and true partner in this work,

The team at Moody, especially Judy, Ashley, Holly, and Erik P.,

Michelle, whose illustrations bring this book to life,

And finally, the membership of Small Brick Church. May we always stay close to our roots.

DO YOU LONG TO LIVE THE LIFE HE CREATED FOR YOU?

Is your identity based on a role? Is it linked to a relationship? Do your achievements influence how you view yourself? What does your family say about you? Who are you as a woman?

Honestly, these are not the right questions. The real question is, who are you as a person created in God's image? Until we see our identity in His, we're settling for seconds. And we were made for so much more . . .